Mark's Story

Philip K. Gladden

Parson's Porch Books

Mark's Story
ISBN: Softcover 978-1-960326-18-8
Copyright © 2023 by Philip K. Gladden

Parson's Porch Books is an imprint of Parson's Porch *&* Company (PP*&*C) in Cleveland, Tennessee. PP*&*C is a self-funded charity which earns money by publishing books of noted authors, representing all genres. Its face and voice is **David Russell Tullock** (dtullock@parsonsporch.com).

Parson's Porch *&* Company *turns books into bread & milk* by sharing its profits with the poor.

www.parsonsporch.com

Mark's Story

This work is

dedicated to the saints
at the Wallace Presbyterian Church,
Wallace, North Carolina,
who love to hear the story
of Jesus and his love,
with thanks for their gracious gift
of a sabbatical leave,
June – September 2018.

Purpose

If asked to tell the story of Jesus, my hunch is most people would use stories, teachings, sayings, and events from Matthew, Luke, and John, even if they couldn't tell you from which gospel the stories came. We tend to make a mishmash of the gospels. Think about Christmas pageants, cards, and carols which have the shepherds following the star and the wise men showing up at the manger at the same time as the shepherds. In addition, Mark's gospel doesn't seem to lend itself to our "telling" of the story of Jesus. Many of the most familiar and beloved stories about and from Jesus can't be found in Mark's story, but Mark is a storyteller *par excellence*. Nevertheless, just as Mark begins his story abruptly with John the Baptist and Jesus appearing on the scene full grown and ready to begin their ministries, he also ends his story in an abrupt manner:

καὶ ἐξελθοῦσαι ἔφυγον απὸ τοῦ μνημείου, εἶχεν γὰρ αὐτὰς τρόμο ς καὶ ἔκστασις καὶ οὐδενὶ οὐδεν εἶπαν, ἐφοβοῦντο γάρ. (Mark 16:8)

And when they went out, they fled from the tomb, for trembling and amazement had them; and they said nothing to no one, for they were afraid.

Yes, Bibles include verses 9 – 20 at the end of Mark, but I am convinced that Mark ended his gospel with verse 8. What a strange ending – "They said nothing to no one, for they were afraid" – to a story whose purpose is to tell "the good news of Jesus Christ Son of God." (Mark 1:1)

This mysterious and abrupt ending of Mark's gospel and the immediacy of his story are the two main characteristics of this narrative account that captured my attention a few years ago. When I was in seminary at Union Theological Seminary in Virginia (now Union Presbyterian Seminary) from 1979-1983, and again when I was working on my Ph.D. in New Testament Biblical Studies (also at Union) from 1986-1991, I was immersed in the historical-critical method of biblical exegesis. The discipline of "narrative criticism" of the Bible was just being developed. If this new discipline of interpretation was mentioned at all, it was in passing and somewhat disparagingly.

But Mark tells a story – "the greatest story ever told!" – and his story deserves to be read, heard, and interpreted as such. The third characteristic of the gospel that fascinates me is that Mark was the first gospel written, around 65 C.E. Although not all scholars agree with this claim of Marcan priority, a convincing case can be made. Because Mark's gospel is first, the questions of *Why? How? For what purpose?* and *For what use?* naturally arise. This present project focuses on the latter question.

In worship, we are accustomed to hearing discrete stories, even verses, isolated from the larger context and story of Mark. However, friends and colleagues have shared their thrilling experiences of hearing accomplished speakers, without use of props and costumes, tell Mark's gospel story in one sitting. To a person, each of the hearers reports the power conveyed through the words of Mark's story. Surely Mark's story was originally intended to be heard in one sitting in worship and other settings in early Christian communities. How much more, then, we can gain from reading and hearing Mark's gospel as a story.

TRANSLATION

During my ministerial sabbatical leave (June – September 2018), I translated the gospel of Mark from the original Koine Greek. I used the following sources:

• *The Greek New Testament (Third Edition),* eds. Kurt Aland, Matthew Black, Carlo M. Martini, Bruce M. Metzger, and Allen Wikgren (New York: United Bible Societies, 1975)

- *A Concise Greek-English Dictionary of the New Testament*, Prepared by Barclay M. Newman, Jr. (at the back of *The Greek New Testament (Third Edition)*)
- Various Greek grammars, to work out translations, to understand idioms, and to learn more about Koine Greek
- "Daily Dose of Greek" website – videos of translation of Mark, for consultation, learning more Koine Greek in-depth, translation comparisons

I did not consult any English language translation of the gospel of Mark. Unless otherwise indicated, all translations are my own.

Presentation

I hope this two-part presentation of Mark's story will be readable and enjoyable. The first part consists of my translation of Mark from Koine Greek to English. It is not a literal/wooden translation, but I do try to maintain Mark's style and some of the interesting characteristics of the Koine Greek language that are not noticeable in an English translation.

As you read this version of Mark's story, you will notice superscript numbers throughout, indicating footnotes. You may certainly read the story without referring to the footnotes. They are not intended to interrupt your enjoyment of Mark's story. However, I will use footnotes to comment on my translation, to call attention to important points to consider, and to recall and to look ahead to other parts of the story.

This translation of Mark's story may include some awkward phrasings (at least to us English speakers) to demonstrate Mark's Greek usage (e.g., the use of the double negative in Mark 16:8, "they told nothing to no one." That's how people talk where I come from!).

Also, I intend for my translation to maintain and convey Mark's sense of urgency and immediacy. Mark repeatedly uses the word εὐθὺς, (immediately), especially in the first half of the story. In my narrative interpretation, I used words and phrases that are synonyms for *immediately*. You might want to keep a list of them. How many can you find? You will also notice the interesting use of what is called *the historical present*. In an effort to give the sense of an excited and motivated storyteller, I will try to stay true to the Greek words (e.g., "and then Jesus says . . .; and then the disciples get in the boat . . .") These phrases are typically translated in the "past" tense in English, which is more pleasing to the hearer's ears. However, this historical present can help you imagine the dynamic character of hearing Mark's story for the first time.

The second part of this presentation of Mark's story is my narrative retelling of my translation of Mark's story from Koine Greek to English. This rendition does not include chapter and verse numbers. While that may be reminiscent of Eugene Peterson's original version of *The Message*, I did not intend to recreate his version of Mark. Instead, I tried to imagine listening to someone tell Mark's story, either in the late first century or early second century or even in the twenty-first century. How would the storyteller keep your attention? What parts of the story would be emphasized? How much would the storyteller assume you as the hearer already know? While I tried to stick as close to my Greek/English translation as possible and not add many extra words or ideas, occasionally I did throw in some interpretive remarks.

There is an old story told about how we came to have chapters and verses in the Bible. As the story goes, a man was riding a horse as he was translating the Bible. Each time he hit a small bump and his pencil jumped, that became a new verse. Each time he hit a big bump, that became a new chapter. Sometimes it seems as if that is as good an explanation of the chapters and verses in the Bible as any other, especially in the letters of the apostle Paul. Reading Mark's story as a complete story, from start to finish, might be a new experience for you. Perhaps reading his story this way will help you understand better Mark's purpose for writing his story about Jesus and how he artfully structures his story.

YOUR RESPONSIBILITY AS A READER AND HEARER OF MARK'S STORY

Mark will make you privy to inside information that other characters in the gospel do not yet know (e.g., Mark 1:1). Pay attention!

Listen to the narrator's (Mark's) voice throughout the gospel. What is the narrator/Mark telling you? Why?

Think of Mark's story more as a portrait than a snapshot. Mark skillfully paints his portrait of who Jesus is and what Jesus means for your life. What do you see? Who is Jesus in Mark's gospel? Who is Jesus in your life?

Finally, remember what Jesus himself says in Mark 4:9: Ὃς ἔχει ὦτα ἀκούειν ἀκουέτω. (The one who has ears let him hear.).

Enjoy!

TRANSLATION FROM GREEK TEXT

CHAPTER 1

1:1   The beginning of the gospel (which means "good news") of Jesus Christ Son of God.[1]

1:2   Just as it has been written in the prophet Isaiah,

> "Look I am sending my messenger before
>
> you, who will prepare your way;

1:3   a voice (is) crying in the wilderness,

> 'Prepare the way of the Lord,
>
> make straight his paths.'"

1:4   John, who was baptizing, came in the wilderness and was proclaiming a baptism of repentance for the forgiveness of sins.

1:5   And[2] the whole region of Judea was going out to him and all the Jerusalemites, and they were baptized by him in the Jordan River after confessing their sins.

1:6   And John was wearing hairs of a camel and a belt of leather around his waist, and was eating locusts and wild honey.

1:7   And he preached and said, "He who is stronger than I is coming after me, of whom I am not worthy, having stooped down, to untie the straps of his sandals;

1:8   I have baptized you with water, but he will baptize you with Holy Spirit."

1:9   And it happened in those days Jesus came from Nazareth of Galilee and was baptized in the Jordan by John.

1:10   And immediately[3] as he was coming up from the water, he saw the heavens split and the Spirit descending on him like a dove.

1:11   And a voice came from the heavens, "You are my Beloved Son, in you I am pleased."[4]

1:12   And immediately the Spirit drives[5] him out into the wilderness.

1:13   And he was in the wilderness forty days being tempted by (the) Satan, and he was in the company of the wild animals, and the angels were giving care to him.

1:14   After John had been arrested Jesus went into Galilee in order to preach the good news/gospel of God[6]

1:15   and was saying, "The time has been fulfilled and the kingdom of God has come near; y'all[7] repent and y'all believe in the good news."

1:16   And as he was passing by the Sea of Galilee, he saw Simon and Andrew the brother of Simon who were casting nets into the sea; for they were fishermen.

1:17   And Jesus said to them, "Come after me/Follow me, and I will make you to become fishers of people."

1:18   And immediately, when they had left their fishing nets behind, they followed him.

1:19   And after he had gone on only a little, he noticed James the son of Zebedee and John his brother, who were in the boat mending the fishing nets,

1:20   And immediately he called them. And after they had left their father Zebedee in the boat with the hired laborers they went after him.

1:21   And they went into Capernaum. And immediately on the sabbath when he had gone into the synagogue he began to teach.

1:22   And they were amazed at his teaching, for he was teaching them as one who has authority and not as the scribes.

1:23   And immediately there was in their synagogue a man with an unclean spirit, and he cried out

1:24   and said, "What have you to do with us, Jesus Nazarene? Have you come to destroy us? I know who you are, the holy one of God."[8]

1:25   And Jesus commanded him by saying, "Be silenced and come out from him!"

1:26   And when the unclean spirit had thrown him into convulsions and cried out with a loud voice, he went out from him.

1:27   And all were amazed, so as to question among themselves and say, "What is this? A new teaching, with authority; he even commands the unclean spirits and they obey him."

1:28   And the report about him immediately went out everywhere into the whole surrounding region of Galilee.

1:29   And immediately after they had gone out from the synagogue they went to the house of Simon and Andrew with James and John.

1:30   And the mother-in-law of Simon was sick with a fever, and immediately they tell him about her.

1:31   And he went and raised her up by taking hold of her hand; and the fever left her, and she began to wait on them.

1:32   When evening had come, when the sun was setting, they were bringing to him all who were sick and demon-possessed.

1:33   And the whole city was gathering at the door.

1:34   And he healed many who were ill with diseases of various kinds, and he cast out many demons, and he did not allow the demons to talk, because they knew him.[9]

1:35   And early in the morning long before daylight when he had gotten up, he went out and went away to a lonely place and there he was praying.

1:36   And Simon searched diligently for him along with those who were with him,

1:37   and they found him and they say to him, "Everyone is looking for you."

1:38   And he says to them, "Let us go elsewhere into the neighboring country towns, in order that I might also preach there; for this reason I have come."

1:39   And he went to preach in their synagogues in all Galilee and to cast out demons.

1:40   And a leper comes to him and begs him, and as he kneels, he says to him, "If you wish to cleanse[10] me, you are able."

1:41   And because he was moved with compassion, when he had stretched out his hand, he touched and said to him, "I wish; be cleansed."

1:42   And immediately the leprosy went out from him, and he was cleansed.

1:43   And when he had spoken harshly to him/commanded him he sent him away,

1:44   and says to him, "Take care that you say nothing to no one[11], but go and show yourself to the priest and offer for your cleansing that which Moses commanded, as a testimony to them."

1:45   But he went out and began to proclaim much and to spread the word/story/message so that he [Jesus] was no longer able openly to enter a city, but was out in the deserted places; and they were coming to him from all directions.

NOTES

[1]The phrase "of Jesus Christ" can mean "The good news *about* Jesus Christ" or "The good news that Jesus Christ *brings*." Does it have to be one or the other? Maybe it's both!

[2]You may have been taught that it is improper to begin sentences with the word "And." However, this was a common practice in Koine Greek and served to move the story along. Editors of English translations don't often include the "And's" at the beginnings of verses.

[3]Mark uses the word εὐθύς no less than forty times in his gospel, eleven times in the first chapter alone. This word communicates a sense of urgency to Mark's message and describes the immediacy of Jesus' mission. See Mark 1:14-15.

[4]As the reader, you already know Jesus is God's Son, because Mark/the narrator told you that in Mark 1:1!

[5]This is the first example of "the historical present." Most English translations (if not all) will translate this as "The Spirit was driving him out into the wilderness," which is a good and correct translation. Using the present tense, however, may give you a sense of a storyteller excitedly telling you about Jesus being sent into the wilderness.

[6]Compare Mark 1:1 – "The beginning of the good news/gospel of Jesus Christ Son of God." – and footnote 1.

[7]In English, it is hard to distinguish "you" (singular) and "you" (plural), except maybe according to context. "Y'all" clearly shows that Jesus is talking to lots of people!

[8]Take note that the demons in Mark's story know who Jesus is (and their identification of him matches what Mark has already told you in Mark 1:1).

[9]See note 8.

[10] "Cleanse" here means more than just making the leprosy go away. The word also means "declare me ritually acceptable." This means the man could be received back into his community.

[11]Here is an example of Mark's use of the double negative – "Don't say anything to anyone!" Jesus' command to the leper to "tell no one nothing" is puzzling. Doesn't Jesus want people to know about him? Referred to by many as "the Messianic secret," this reluctance on Jesus' part for people to say who he is seems to be related to the wide range of opinions people held about him (see Mark 8:28), Jesus' own message about what kind of Messiah he is, and Mark's point that, unless you can accept Jesus as the suffering Son of Man, you will misunderstand him (see Peter's reaction in Mark 8:32).

CHAPTER 2

2:1   And after he had come again into Capernaum some days later it was heard that he was in a house.

2:2   And many people were gathered, so as no longer to be room nor places at the door, and he was telling them the word/message.

2:3   And they came bearing to him a paralytic who was taken up by four men.

2:4   And because they were not able to bear [him] to him on account of the crowd they unroofed the roof where he was, and after gouging out they lowered the stretcher where the paralytic was lying.

2:5   And when Jesus sees their faith he says to the paralytic, "My child, your sins are forgiven."

2:6   But some of the scribes were sitting there and wondering in their hearts,

2:7   "Why is this one speaking in this way? He blasphemes; who is able to forgive sins except the one God?"

2:8   And immediately when/because Jesus knew in his spirit that they were questioning in this way in themselves, he says to them, "Why are you questioning these things in your hearts?

2:9   Which is easier, to say to the paralytic, 'Your sins are forgiven,' or to say, 'Get up and take up your stretcher and walk'?

2:10   but in order that you might know that the Son of Man has authority on the earth to forgive sins" – he says to the paralytic,

2:11   "I say to you, get up, take up your stretcher and go to your house."

2:12   And when he had gotten up and immediately taken up the stretcher he went out before all of them, so that they all were amazed and glorified God, and said, "We have never seen of such kind."

2:13   And he went out again beside the sea; and the whole crowd was coming to him, and he began to teach them.

2:14   And as he passed by, he saw Levi the son of Alphaeus who was sitting in the tax office, and he says to him, "Follow me." And when he had stood up, he followed him.

2:15   And it happened that he was sitting at table in the house, and many tax collectors and sinners were eating with Jesus and his disciples; for there were many of them and they were following him.

2:16   And when the scribes of the Pharisees saw that he was eating with the sinners and tax collectors they began to say to his disciples, "Why is he eating with the tax collectors and sinners?"

2:17   And when he heard, Jesus says to them, "The well people don't need a physician but those who are sick; I have not come to call righteous people but sinners."

2:18   And the disciples of John were fasting. And they come and they say to him, "Why do the disciples of John and the disciples of the Pharisees fast, but your disciples do not fast?"

2:19   And Jesus said to them, "The sons of the bridegroom are not able to fast while the bridegroom is with them, are they? As long as they have the bridegroom with them, they are not able to fast;

2:20   but days are coming, when the bridegroom is taken from them, and they will fast in that day.

2:21   No one sews a piece of unshrunk cloth on an old garment, otherwise the fullness takes away from it, the new from the old, and the tear becomes worse.

2:22   And no one puts new wine into old wineskins – otherwise, the wine will burst the wineskins, and both the wine and the skins will be lost – but new wine into new wineskins."

2:23   And it happened as he was going through the grainfields on the sabbath, his disciples began to make a way by plucking the heads of grain.

2:24   And the Pharisees were saying to him, "Look, why are they doing on the sabbath what it is not lawful to do?"

2:25   And he says to them, "Have you never read what David did, when he had a need and was hungry, he and the ones with him?

2:26   How he went into the house of God when Abiathar was the high priest and ate the bread offered to God, which it is not lawful for anyone to eat except the priests, and he gave it also to the ones who were with him?"

2:27   And he was saying to them, "The sabbath was made for humanity and not humanity for the sabbath;

2:28   therefore the Son of Man is lord even of the sabbath."

CHAPTER 3

3:1 And he entered into the synagogue again. And there was a man there who had a withered hand;

3:2 And they were watching him closely whether he will heal on the sabbath, in order that they might bring charges against him.

3:3 And he says to the man who has the withered hand, "Get up! Come into the middle!"

3:4 And he says to them, "Is it lawful on the sabbath to do good or to do evil, to preserve life or to kill?" But they were silent.

3:5 And when he had looked around at them with anger, because he was deeply grieved at the stubbornness of their heart, he said to the man, "Stretch out your hand." And he stretched it out, and his hand was restored.

3:6 And when the Pharisees had gone out, immediately they were establishing a plan with the Herodians against him that they might kill him.

3:7 And Jesus with his disciples withdrew to the sea; and a great crowd from Galilee followed him; and from Judea

3:8 and from Jerusalem and from Idumea and beyond the Jordan and near Tyre and Sidon, a great crowd came to him because they heard how much he was doing.

3:9 And he said to his disciples that a boat might be ready for him on account of the crowd in order that it [the crowd] might not crush him.

3:10 Then he healed many, so as to press close to him in order that they might touch him, as many had diseases.

3:11   And the unclean spirits, whenever they were seeing him, were falling down before him and crying out, "You are the Son of God!"[1]

3:12   And he insistently was commanding them that they not make him known.[2]

3:13   And he goes up on the mountain and calls those he wanted, and they went to him.

3:14   And he appointed twelve, [whom he also named apostles,] that they might be with him and that he might send them to preach

3:15   and to have authority to cast out demons.

3:16   [and he appointed the twelve] and he gave Simon the name Peter,

3:17   and he appointed James the son of Zebedee and John the brother of James, and he gave them the name Boanerges, which is Sons of Thunder;

3:18   and (he appointed) Andrew and Philip and Bartholomew and Matthew and Thomas and James the son of Alphaeus and Thaddeus and Simon the Cananaean

3:19   and Judas Iscariot[3], who also betrayed him.

3:20   And he comes into a house; and again, the crowd comes together so that they were not able even to eat a meal.[4]

3:21   And when his family heard they came to seize him, for they were saying that he was out of his mind.

3:22   And the scribes who had come down from Jerusalem were saying, "He has Beelzebul," and "By the ruler of demons he is casting out demons."

3:23   And after he had summoned them, he was speaking to them in parables, "How is it possible for Satan to cast out Satan?

3:24   And if a kingdom is divided against itself, that kingdom is not able to stand.

3:25   And if a house is divided against itself, that house is not able to stand.

3:26   And if Satan stands against himself and is divided, he is not able to stand but has an end.

3:27   But no one is not able[5] to enter into the strong man's house and plunder his goods unless first he binds the strong man, and then he will plunder his house.

3:28   Truly I say to you that all sins and whatever blasphemies they might blaspheme will be forgiven to the sons of men;

3:29   but whoever blasphemes against the Holy Spirit does not have forgiveness forever[6], but is guilty of an eternal sin" –

3:30   because they were saying, "He has an unclean spirit."

3:31   And his mother and his brothers come and while they are standing outside, they sent to him calling him.

3:32   And a crowd was sitting around him, and they say to him, "Behold your mother and your brothers [and your sisters] are outside looking for you."

3:33   And he answered them and said, "Who is my mother and my brothers?"

3:34   And when he looked around at those sitting in a circle around him, he says, "Look, my mother and my brothers.

3:35   For whoever does the will of God, that one is my brother and sister and mother."

NOTES

[1]Here is another example of the demons correctly identifying who Jesus is with information you already know from Mark 1:1.

[2]Compare this command to Jesus' command to the leper to be silent in Mark 1:44.

[3]In Hebrew, *ish Karioth* which means "the man from Karioth."

[4]The phrase "to eat a meal" is literally "to eat bread." This is an example of *synecdoche*, "a part of the whole."

[5]Here is another example of the double negative – "No one is able . . ."

[6] "Does not have forgiveness forever" is a way of saying "will never have forgiveness."

CHAPTER 4

4:1   And again he began to teach beside the sea. And a great crowd gathers to him, so that after he had gotten into a boat he sat on the sea, and the crowd was beside the sea on the land.

4:2   And he was teaching them many things with parables[1], and he was saying to them with his teaching,

4:3   "Listen! Look, the sower went out to sow.

4:4   And it happened while he was sowing some fell beside the road, and the birds came and ate it.

4:5   And other fell on rocky ground where it did not have much soil, and it immediately sprouted because it did not have depth of soil;

4:6   and when the sun rose it was scorched, and because it did not have roots it withered.

4:7   And other fell among the thorn-plants, and the thorn-plants grew up and choked them, and they did not give fruit.

4:8   And others fell in the good earth, and were giving fruit. It grew up and reached full growth and produced one thirty and one sixty and one one hundred."

4:9   And he was saying, "Whoever has ears to hear, let him hear!"[2]

4:10   And when he was alone, the ones around him with the twelve were asking him about the parables.

4:11   And he was saying to them, "To you the mystery of the kingdom of God has been given; but to those who are outside all things are in parables

4:12   so that

'Although seeing they might see and yet not know,

and although hearing they might hear and yet not understand,

lest they turn and it might be forgiven to them."'[3]

4:13   And he says to them, "Do you not know this parable? And how will you understand all the parables?

4:14   The sower is sowing the word.

4:15   Now these are the ones beside the road where the word is sown, and whenever they hear, immediately Satan comes and snatches the word which has been sown among them.

4:16   And these are the ones sown on rocky ground, who whenever they hear the word immediately they receive it with joy,

4:17   and they do not have a root among themselves but are temporary; then when trouble or persecution happens on account of the word immediately they fall into sin/fall away.

4:18   And others are those sown in the thorn-plants; these are the ones who have heard the word,

4:19   and the cares of the present life and the deception of wealth and the desires for other things enter in and choke out the word, and it becomes unfruitful.

4:20   and those are the ones sown on the good soil, who hear the word and receive it and bear fruit, one thirty and one sixty, and one one hundred."

4:21   And he was saying to them, "Is a lamp brought in order that it might be placed under the basket or the bed? Or in order that it might be placed on the lampstand?

4:22   For it is not hidden except that it might be revealed nor is it stored away but that it might be brought out into the open.

4:23   If anyone has ears to hear, let him hear!"[4]

4:24   And he was saying to them, "Watch out what you hear. In what measure you measure out it will be measured to you and added to you.

4:25   For whoever has, it will be given to him; and whoever does not have, even that which he has will be taken from him."

4:26   And he was saying, "Thus is the kingdom of God like a man who sows seed on the ground

4:27   and he sleeps and rises night and day, and the seed sprouts and grows, how he himself does not know.

4:28   The earth on its own[5] is productive, first a stalk, then a head of grain, then the full grain in the head of grain/mature grain.

4:29   but whenever the crop is ripe, immediately he sends for the sickle, because the harvest has arrived."

4:30   And he was saying, "How might we liken the kingdom of God, or by what parable might we describe it?

4:31   As to a mustard seed, which whenever it is sown upon the earth although the smallest of all the seeds which are sown upon the earth,

4:32   and whenever it is sown it grows up and becomes greater than all the garden plants and makes large branches, so that the wild birds of the air are able to nest under its shade."

4:33   And he used to speak the word to them by means of many such parables, just as they were able to hear;

4:34   but without a parable he was not speaking to them, but in private he was explaining all things to his own disciples.

4:35   And he says to them in that day when evening had come, "Let us cross over to the other side."

4:36   And when they had left the crowd, they take him as he was in the boat, and other boats were with him.

4:37   And a great storm of wind arises, and the waves were beating against the boat, so that already the boat was filling up.

4:38   And he was in the stern sleeping on a cushion; and they wake him up and say to him, "Teacher, is it of no concern to you that we are perishing?"

4:39   And after he had awakened, he commanded the wind and said to the sea, "Calm down, be silent!" And the wind ceased, and there was a great calm.

4:40   And he said to them, "Why are you afraid? [6] Do you not yet have faith?"

4:41   And they were frightened (with) a great fear, and they were saying to one another, "Who then is this one that even the wind and the sea obey him?"

NOTES

[1]Mark's gospel does not include many parables of Jesus. This may be because the gospel is the shortest of the four. Whatever the reason, because Mark includes so few parables, pay attention to the ones he does include.

[2]The second use of the word "hear" is in the imperative, so the sense of what Jesus says is, "Make sure you understand! You'd better listen!"

[3]See Isaiah 6:9-10.

[4]See note 2.

[5]The Greek word is αὐτομάτη from which we get the word "automatic."

[6]Another way to translate "Why are you afraid?" is "Why are you cowardly?"

CHAPTER 5

5:1   And they went to the other side of the sea into the country/region of the Gerasenes.

5:2   And immediately as he was getting out of the boat a man from the tombs with an unclean spirit met him,

5:3   who lived among the tombs; and no chains nor anyone was able any longer to bind him,

5:4   for he had often been bound with foot chains and shackles and the shackles had been torn apart by him and the foot chains had been shattered, and no one was able to subdue him;

5:5   and all night and day in and among the tombs and in the mountains, he was crying out/he used to cry out and bruise himself with stones.

5:6   And when he saw Jesus from far off, he ran and fell down and worshiped him,

5:7   and cried out with a great voice and said, "What business do you and I have, Jesus Son of the Most High God? I beg you God, do not torment me."[1]

5:8   For he was saying to him, "You unclean spirit, come out from the man."

5:9   And he was asking him, "What is your name?" And he said to him, "My name is Legion, for we are many."

5:10   And he was begging him insistently that he might not send them out of the neighborhood.

5:11   Now there near the mountain a large herd of pigs was grazing;

5:12   so he begged him and said, "Send us into the pigs, so that we might go into them."

5:13   So he allowed them. And when the unclean spirits had gone out, they went into the pigs, and the herd rushed down the steep bank into the sea, about 2,000, and they drowned in the sea.

5:14   And the ones who were feeding them fled and told in the city and in the countryside; and they went to see what had happened.

5:15   So they came to Jesus and saw the demon-possessed man sitting, clothed and in his right mind, the one who had had Legion, and they were afraid.

5:16   And the ones who saw what had happened to the demon-possessed man also told them about the pigs.

5:17   And they began to beg him to go away from their boundaries.

5:18   And as he was getting into the boat, the man who had been demon-possessed begged him, that he might go with him.

5:19   And he did not allow him, but said to him, "Go to your house and to your own people and tell them all/how much the Lord has done for you and has shown kindness to you."

5:20   So he went out and began to proclaim in the Decapolis how much Jesus had done for him, and all were amazed.

5:21   And after Jesus had again crossed over in the boat to the other side, a large crowd came together in his presence, and he was beside the sea.

5:22   And one of the presidents/leaders of the synagogue, by the name of Jairus, came, and when he saw him, he fell at his feet[2]

5:23   and he begged him insistently and said[3], "My little daughter is very sick/dying, in order that you might come and might lay your hands on her and she might be saved/healed and live."

5:24   And he went with him. And a great crowd was following him, and pressed upon him/was thronging to him.

5:25   And a woman who had a flow of blood for twelve years –

5:26   -- and because she had suffered severely/much/many things at the hands of many doctors and had spent all of her money and had not gained but rather had gotten worse;

5:27   when she heard about Jesus, she went in the crowd from behind and touched his garment;

5:28   for she was saying, "If I touch at least/even his garments I will be healed/saved/made whole."[4]

5:29   And immediately her flow of blood ceased/was stopped and she knew in her body that she had been cured of her illness.

5:30   And immediately when Jesus perceived in himself that power had gone out from him, he turned and said, "Who touched my clothes?"

5:31   And his disciples were saying to him, "You see the crowd that is pressing upon you, and yet you are saying, 'Who touched me?'"

5:32   And he was looking around to see who had done this.

5:33   So the fearful and trembling woman, because she knew what had happened to her, went and fell down before him and told him the whole truth.[5]

5:34   But he said to her, "Daughter[6], your faith has healed/saved you; go on your way in peace, and be healed/cured from/of your illness."

5:35   While he was still talking, they came from the house of the president/leader of the synagogues and said, "Your daughter has died; why are you still troubling the teacher?"

5:36   But when Jesus overheard the message spoken, he said to the president/leader of the synagogue, "Don't be afraid, only believe!"

5:37   And he did not allow no one[7] to accompany him except Peter and James and John the brother of James.

5:38   And they went into the house of the president/leader of the synagogue and he was seeing confusion and much weeping and wailing,

5:39   and after he went in, he said to them, "Why are you stirred up and weeping? The child has not died but is sleeping."

5:40   And they were laughing at him. But when he had cast them all out, he took the father of the little child and the mother and those with him, and went into where the little child was.

5:41   And when he had taken hold of the hand of the little child, he said to her, "Talitha cum," which means "Get up!"[8]

5:42   And immediately she stood up and began to walk around, for she was twelve years old.[9] And immediately they were amazed with a great amazement.

5:43   And he ordered them strongly/strictly, that no one might know (about) this, and he told them to give her something to eat.

NOTES

[1] "I adjure you in the name of God . . ." The demon is trying to gain the upper hand. Note that the demon knows who Jesus is (cf. Mark 1:1).

²Cf. Mark 5:6: "And when he saw Jesus from far off, he ran and fell down and worshiped him."

³Cf. Mark 5:10: "And he was begging him insistently that he might not send them out of the neighborhood."

⁴Cf. Mark 5:23: "that you might come and might lay your hands on her and she might be saved/healed and live."

⁵Cf. Mark 5:6: "And when he saw Jesus from far off, he ran and fell down and worshiped him." and Mark 5:22: "And one of the presidents/leaders of the synagogue, by the name of Jairus, came, and when he saw him, he fell at his feet"

⁶Cf. Mark 5:23: "My little daughter is very sick," Mark 5:35: "Your daughter has died."

⁷This "double negative" is actually a common and good Greek construction. καὶ οὐκ ἀφῆκεν οὐδένα μετ᾽ αὐτοῦ συνακολουθῆσαι εἰ μὴ τὸν Πέτρον καὶ Ἰάκωβον καὶ Ἰωάννην τὸν ἀδελφὸν Ἰακώβου.

⁸ "Girl, I say to you, get up!" or even "Sweetie, get up!"

⁹Note that the woman had the flow of blood for twelve years. Cf. Mark 5:25: "And a woman who had a flow of blood for twelve years . . ."

CHAPTER 6

6:1   And he went out from there, and he came to his hometown, and his disciples were following him.

6:2   And when the sabbath came, he began to teach in the synagogues; and many, when they heard, were amazed and said, "From where did he get these things, and what is the wisdom given to him and what are such miracles that are coming about by his hands?

6:3   Is this not the builder/carpenter, the son of Mary and the brother of James and Juda(s) and Simon? Are not his sisters here with us?" And they were rejecting/having doubts about him.

6:4   And Jesus was saying to them, "A prophet is not dishonored/without honor except in his hometown and among his relatives and in his house."

6:5   And he was not able to do no miracle[1] there, except by laying his hands on a few sick people he healed them.

6:6   And he was amazed at their unbelief.

6:7   And he summoned the twelve, and began to send them out two by two, and he had given them authority over the unclean spirits;

6:8   and he ordered them/gave them instructions not to take anything on the way except a bag, not bread, not a staff, not money in a belt,

6:9   but putting on sandals and not to put on two cloaks.

6:10   And he was saying to them, "Wherever you go into a house, remain there until you go out from there.

6:11   And whichever place does not receive you nor listen to you, as you are going out from there shake off the dust under your feet as a witness against them."

6:12   And they went out and proclaimed that they should repent,

6:13   and they were casting out many demons and anointing with oil many sick people and healing them.

6:14   And King Herod heard, for his name became known, and they were saying, "John the baptizer has been raised from the dead, and on account of this the deeds of power are at work in him."

6:15   But others were saying, "It is Elijah"; still others were saying, "He is a prophet like one of the prophets."

6:16   But when Herod heard this (about Jesus), he was saying, "John, whom I beheaded, has been raised."

6:17   For Herod himself, when he had sent for him, arrested John and bound him in prison on account of Herodias, the wife of his brother, Philip, because he married her;

6:18   for John was saying to Herod, "It is not lawful for you to have the wife of your brother."

6:19   So Herodias was hostile towards him and was wishing to kill him, and she was not able;

6:20   for Herod feared John, because he knew he was a righteous and holy man, so he was protecting him, and although when he heard him, he was greatly perplexed, yet he was also listening to him gladly.

6:21   And an opportune day arrived when Herod gave a feast for his birthday celebration for his persons of high status and high-ranking officials and prominent people of Galilee.

6:22   And when his daughter by Herodias came in and danced, she pleased Herod and his guests. The king said to the girl, "Ask me whatever you wish, and I will give it to you."

6:23   And he swore to her strongly, "Whatever you ask of me I will give to you, to the point of half of my kingdom."

6:24   And she went out and said to her mother, "What shall I ask for?" She said, "The head of John who was baptizing."

6:25   And she went in immediately with haste to the king and asked him and said, "I wish for you right now to give me the head of John the baptizer."

6:26   And, although the king was very sad, because of the oaths and the dinner guests, he did not want to refuse her;

6:27   and immediately the king sent and commanded the executioner to bring his head. And he went out and decapitated him in the prison.

6:28   And he carried his head on a platter and gave it to the girl, and the little girl gave it to her mother.

6:29   And when his disciples heard, they came and took his corpse and placed it in a grave.

6:30   And the apostles met with Jesus and told him all the things which they had done and which they had taught.

6:31   And he said to them, "Come you yourselves privately to a deserted place and rest a little." For the ones coming and going were many, and they did not have an opportunity to eat.

6:32   And they went away in the boat to a deserted place alone.

6:33   And the people saw them departing, and many recognized them, and by foot from all of the cities they were running there and got there ahead of them.

6:34   And when he got out, he saw a great crowd, and he was moved with compassion for them because they were like sheep without a shepherd, so he began to teach them many things.

6:35   And when it already got late, his disciples came to him and said, "The place is deserted, and already the hour is late.

6:36   Send them away, so that going into the surrounding fields and villages, they might buy for themselves what they might eat."

6:37   But he said to them, "How many loaves do you have? Go, see." And when they found out they said, "Five, and two fish."

6:38   So Jesus answered and said to them, "You give them something to eat." And they said to him, "Are we to go away and buy two hundred denarii of bread and give it to them to eat?"

6:39   And he commanded them to seat all in groups on the green grass.

6:40   So they sat down in groups[2] in hundreds and by fifties.

6:41   And after he took the five loaves and the two fish and looked up into heaven, he blessed/asked a blessing on the food and tore the loaves into pieces and gave them to his disciples in order that they might distribute (the loaves) to them and he apportioned the two fish to all.

6:42   And all ate and were satisfied.

6:43   And they took up fragments filling twelve baskets, also of the fish.

6:44   And the ones who ate the loaves were 5,000 men.[3]

6:45   And immediately he took his disciples to get into the boat and go ahead of him to the other side to Bethsaida, while he sent the crowd away.

6:46   And when he had said goodbye to them, he went away to the mountain to pray.

6:47   And when evening came, the boat was in the middle of the sea, and he was alone on the land.

6:48   And when he saw them straining in the rowing, for the wind was against them, about the fourth watch of the night[4] he came to them walking on the sea; and he wanted to pass them by.

6:49   But when they saw him walking on the sea, they thought he was a ghost, and they cried out;

6:50   for all saw him and were terrified. But he immediately spoke with them and said, "I am[5]; do not be afraid."

6:51   And he came up to them in the boat, and the wind ceased. And they were utterly amazed among themselves,

6:52   for they did not understand about the loaves, but their heart was stubborn.

6:53   And when they had crossed over to the land, they came to Gennesaret and they were moored.

6:54   And when they got out of the boat, immediately they recognized him

6:55   and were running about that whole territory and began to carry on the stretchers those who were sick to where they heard that he was.

6:56   And wherever he went into a village or a city or a field, they placed the sick in the marketplaces, and they were begging him that they might at least touch the hem of his garment[6]; and whoever touched it/him was being saved/healed.

NOTES

[1]This is another example of the common "double negative" – καὶ **οὐκ ἐδύνατο** ἐκεῖ **ποιῆσαι οὐδεμίαν** δύναμιν, εἰ μὴ ὀλίγοις ἀρρώστοις ἐπιθεὶς τὰς χεῖρας ἐθεράπευσεν.

[2]The Greek phrase for "in groups" is πρασιαὶ πρασιαὶ, the dative plural of πρασιά, which literally means "garden plot." Here's a delightful image of people sitting row by row in green grass, "people planted in green grass."

[3]The Greek word used here for "people" in many English translations is ἄνδρες which is the masculine plural of the noun ἀνήρ. That noun is translated as "man, husband," which means it definitely refers to a male person. Thus, ἄνδρες means "men." The Greek noun ἄνθρωπος (plural – ἄνθρωποι) can be translated as "man/men," but is also used more generally to mean "human being/person." Since Mark specifically uses ἄνδρες, it is reasonable to assume there were also women and children present at the feeding that day. How many were actually in the crowd? Otherwise, you have to wonder why 5,000 men were gathered in one deserted place.

[4]3:00 – 6:00 a.m.

[5]The Greek phrase ἐγώ εἰμι can be translated "It is I." Literally it is translated "I am," which evokes God's name as revealed to Moses in Exodus 3:14: God said to Moses, "I AM WHO I AM." He said further, "Thus you shall say to the Israelites, 'I AM has sent me to you.'" I AM = YHWH (in Hebrew)

[6]Cf. Mark 5:28 in the story about the woman with the flow of blood: "for she was saying, "If I touch at least/even his garments I will be healed/saved/made whole."

CHAPTER 7

7:1   And the Pharisees and some of the scribes who came from Jerusalem gathered to him

7:2   and when they saw that some of his disciples were eating bread with unclean hands, that is not according to ritual law,

7:3   for the Pharisees and all the Jews do not eat unless they wash their hands to the wrist/carefully and in the proper way, and by so doing keep the tradition of the elders,

7:4   and they do not eat from the marketplace unless they wash themselves, and there are many other things which they accept to keep, the ritual washings of cups and of pots and of copper vessels [and of beds] –

7:5   and the Pharisees and the scribes asked him, "Why do your disciples not live/walk according to the tradition of the elders, but eat bread with unclean hands?"

7:6   So he said to them, "Isaiah prophesied correctly about you, as it has been written [that], 'This people honors me with lips, but their heart is very far from me.

7:7   They worship me in vain, because they teach teachings/doctrines (which are) human rules.'

7:8   Forsaking the commandment of God you hold fast a human tradition."

7:9   And he said to them, "You very well make invalid the commandment of God, in order   that you might establish your tradition.

7:10   For Moses said, 'Honor your father and your mother,' and 'The one who speaks evil of/curses father or mother, let him be put to death.'

7:11   But you say, 'If a man says to father or to mother, "Corban," which is "Gift," which if   you   benefited from it,

7:12   you no longer allow him to do anything for the father or the mother,

7:13   thereby canceling the word of God by your tradition which you have handed down,   and   you   are doing/performing many such proverbs."

7:14   And when he again called the crowd to him, he said, "All of you listen to me and understand.

7:15   There is nothing outside of the person which, going into him, is able to defile him; but the things that come out of a person are the things that defile a person.

7:16   (omitted) "If anyone has ears to hear, let him listen."

7:17   And when he went into the house (away) from the crowd, his disciples were asking   him (about) the parable.

7:18   And he said to them, "In the same way are you also without understanding? Do you not understand that everything from without that goes into the person is unable to defile him

7:19   because it does not enter into his heart but into his stomach, and it goes into the latrine?" – declaring all things ritually clean.

7:20   So he was saying to them, "That which goes out of a person, that defiles the person,

7:21   for from within the human heart come evil thoughts, sexual immorality, thefts, murders,

7:22   adulteries, covetousness, wickedness, deceit, sensuality, envy, blasphemy, arrogance, foolishness;

7:23   all these things come out from within and defile the person."

7:24   So after he arose, he departed from there and went away into the region(s) of Tyre.

And when he went into a house, he did not want anyone to know, but/and he was not able to escape notice.

7:25   But immediately when a woman whose daughter had an unclean spirit heard about him, she came and fell down at his feet;[1]

7:26   now the woman was Greek/Gentile, a Syrophoenician by race; and she asked him that he might cast out the demon from her daughter.

7:27   And he was saying to her, "Let the children be satisfied first, for it is not good/right to take the bread of the children and throw it to the dogs."

7:28   But she answered and said, "[Yes,] Lord, but even the little dogs underneath the table eat from the crumbs of the little children."

7:29   And he said to her, "On account of this word/what you said, go, the demon has gone out from your daughter."

7:30   And after she went away to her house, she found the little girl lying on the bed and the demon cast out.

7:31   And again he went out from the region(s) of Tyre and he went through Sidon to the Sea of Galilee in the midst of the region(s) of the Decapolis.

7:32   And they brought to him a deaf and mute man, and they begged him that he might lay his hand on him.

7:33   And after he took him aside from the crowd privately, he put his fingers in his ears and after he spat, he touched his tongue,

7:34   and after he looked up to heaven, he groaned, and said to him, "Ephatha," which is "Be opened!"

7:35 And immediately his ears were opened, and the bond of his tongue was loosened, and he was speaking correctly.

7:36 And he ordered them that they might tell no one; but as much as he was commanding them, all the more exceedingly they were proclaiming.

7:37 And they were completely, exceedingly amazed, saying "He has done all things well; he even makes the deaf to hear and the mute to talk."

NOTES

[1]Cf. Mark 5:6; 5:22; 5:33.

CHAPTER 8

8:1   In those days, when there again was a great crowd and they did not have anything to eat, when he summoned his disciples, he said to them,

8:2   "I am moved with pity for the crowd because already they have been with me for three days and they do not have anything to eat;

8:3   and if I send them away hungry to their houses, they will grow faint on the road; and some of them have come from far off."

8:4   And his disciples answered him, "How/from where will anyone be able to feed them loaves in a deserted place?"

8:5   And he was asking them, "How many loaves do you have?" And they said, "Seven."

8:6   And he commanded the crowd to sit on the ground; and after he took the seven loaves and gave thanks, he broke (them) and was giving them to his disciples that they might distribute them and put them before the crowd.

8:7   They also had a few small fish; and when he blessed them, he said to distribute them also.

8:8   And they ate and were filled, and they took up seven baskets of an abundance of fragments.

8:9   Now there were about four thousand men. And he released them.[1]

8:10   And immediately after he got into the boat with his disciples, he went into the region of Dalmanutha.

8:11   And the Pharisees went out and began to question him/dispute or argue with him, by seeking from him a sign from heaven, in order to test him/because they were testing him.

8:12 And when he gave a deep groan in his spirit, he said, "Why does this generation seek a sign? Truly I say to you, if a sign will be given to this generation . . ."[2]

8:13 And after he left them and again had embarked, he went over to the other side.

8:14 And they forgot to take bread and, except for one loaf, they did not have any with them in the boat.

8:15 And he was commanding them by saying, "Watch out/Look out/Understand, beware of the yeast of the Pharisees and the yeast of Herod."

8:16 And they were discussing with one another that they didn't have any loaves/bread.

8:17 And because he knew he said to them, "Why are you discussing that you do not have   loaves? Do you not yet understand nor comprehend? Do you have your stubborn heart?

8:18 Although you have eyes do you not see and although you have ears do you not hear/understand? Do you not remember?

8:19 When I broke the five loaves for the five thousand, how many baskets full of fragments did you take up?" They said to him, "Twelve."

8:20 When [I broke] the seven [loaves] for the four thousand, how many baskets full of fragments did you take up?" They said to him, "Seven."

8:21 And he was saying to them, "Do you not yet understand?"

8:22 And they came to Bethsaida. And they (different subject) brought a blind man to him and begged him that he might/would touch him.

8:23   And after he took the hand of the blind man, he carried him out away from the village, and after he spat in his eyes and placed his hands on him, he asked him, "What do you see? Do you see anything?"

8:24   And when he regained his sight, he said, "I see people, I see them walking around, as   trees."

8:25   And then, again he placed his hands upon his eyes, and he saw clearly/had his sight restored,   and   he   was cured, and he saw all things clearly.

8:26   And he sent him to his house, saying, "Do not go into the village."

8:27   And Jesus and his disciples went out into the villages of Caesarea Philippi; and on the way he asked his disciples, saying to them, "Who are people saying me to be/that I am?"

8:28   So they said to him by saying (they replied to him), "John the Baptist, and others, Elijah, but others that you are one of the prophets."

8:29   And he was asking them, "But you, who do you say that I am/me to be?" Peter answered and said to him, "You are the Christ/the Anointed One/the Messiah."

8:30   And he charged them that they might talk about him to no-one.

8:31   And he began to teach them that it was necessary[3] for the Son of Man to suffer many things and to be rejected at the hands of the elders and the high priests and the scribes and to be killed and after three days to rise again.

8:32   And he was speaking the word openly. And when Peter took him aside, he began to rebuke him.

8:33   But after he turned and saw his disciples, he rebuked Peter and said, "Get behind me, Satan, because you are not thinking the thoughts of God but the thoughts of humans."

8:34   And when he had summoned the crowd with his disciples, he said to them, "If anyone wishes to follow after me,[4] let him renounce himself and let him take up his cross and let him follow me.

8:35   For whoever wishes to save his life will lose it; but whoever will lose his life for my sake and for the sake of the gospel will save it.

8:36   For what does it profit a person to gain the whole world and to lose/forfeit his life?

8:37   For what can/should a person give up in exchange for his life?

8:38   For whoever is ashamed of me and my words in this unfaithful and sinful generation,   the Son of Man also will be ashamed of him whenever he comes in the glory of his   Father with the holy angels."

NOTES

[1]In Matthew's parallel story, he explicitly states οἱ δὲ ἐσθίοντες ἦσαν τετρακισχίλιοι ἄνδρες χωρὶς γυναικῶν καὶ παιδίων, "And the ones who ate were four thousand men without (not counting) women and children."

[2]This is just the "if" phrase of a conditional statement. Leaving the thought incomplete (no "then" statement) means "This is NOT going to happen!"

[3]dei: - "It is necessary" – the divine necessity, a way to avoid using the divine name of God.

[4]ὀπίσω μου ἀκολουθεῖν. . . "to follow after me." Cf. 8:33 - Ὕπαγε ὀπίσω μου, Σαταν᾽ᾶ:. . . "Get behind me, Satan."

CHAPTER 9

9:1   And he was saying to them, "Truly I say to you, that there are some of those standing here who will not taste death until they see the kingdom of God having come with power."

9:2   And after six days, Jesus took along Peter and James and John, and took them to a high mountain privately. And he was transformed before them,

9:3   and his clothes became exceedingly dazzling white such as a bleacher on the earth is not able to bleach in this way.

9:4   And Elijah with Moses appeared to them and they were talking with Jesus.

9:5   And Peter answered/said to Jesus, "Rabbi (Teacher), it is good for us to be here, and let us make three tents, one for you and one for Moses and one for Elijah."

9:6   For he did not know what he was saying, for they were terrified.

9:7   And a cloud came and overshadowed them, and a voice came from the cloud, "This is my Son the beloved, listen to him."

9:8   And suddenly when they looked around, they no longer saw anyone but Jesus alone with them.

9:9   And as they were descending from the mountain, he was commanding them that they should tell no one what they saw, except whenever the Son of Man might rise from the dead.

9:10   And they held the word fast to themselves as they were questioning what is the rising from the dead/what rising from the dead might mean.

9:11   And they were asking him and saying, "Why do the scribes say that it was/is necessary that Elijah come first?"

9:12   So he said, "Indeed since Elijah came first, he restored all things, and how is it written concerning the Son of Man that he should suffer many things and be despised/rejected?

9:13   But I say to you both that Elijah even has come, and they did to him whatever things they were desiring, just as it had been written concerning him."

9:14   And when they returned to the disciples, they saw a large crowd around them and scribes arguing with them.

9:15   And immediately when they saw him, the whole crowd was greatly amazed and they   ran   up   and greeted him.

9:16   And   he   asked   them,   "What   are   you debating/discussing with them?"

9:17   And one from the crowd answered him, "Teacher, I brought my son to you, because he has a spirit of muteness;

9:18   and whenever it attacks him, it dashes him to the ground and he foams at the mouth and grinds his teeth and becomes stiff; and I asked your disciples that they might cast it out, but they were not able."

9:19   So he answered them, "O faithless generation, how long will I be with you? How long will I put up with you? Bring him to me."

9:20   And they brought him to him. And when he saw him, the spirit immediately threw him into convulsions, and when he fell on the ground he rolled around foaming at the mouth.[1]

9:21   And he asked his father, "How much time is it since this happened to him/How long has he been like this?" He said, "From childhood.

9:22   And frequently it threw him into both fire and water that it might kill him; but if something can be done/if you can do anything, help us by having compassion for us."

9:23   So Jesus said to him, "Concerning 'If you are able...' – all things are possible for the one who believes."

9:24   Immediately the father of the child cried out and said, "I believe; help my unbelief."

9:25   So when Jesus saw that a crowd was running together toward them, he rebuked/ commanded the unclean spirit and said to it, "Mute and deaf spirit, I command you, come out from him that you will no longer enter into him."

9:26   And when it had cried out and thrown him into convulsions, it came out; and he became as a dead one, so that many were saying that he had died (many were saying, "He has died.").

9:27   But by taking his hand, Jesus raised him up, and he stood up.

9:28   And after he went into a house, his disciples privately were asking him, "Why were we not able to cast it out?"

9:29   And he said to them, "This kind by no way is able to come out except by prayer."

9:30   And when they went out from there, they were passing through Galilee, and he did not wish anyone to know;

9:31   for he was teaching his disciples and saying to them, "The Son of man is being handed over/will be handed over into human hands, and they will kill him, and when he has been killed, after three days he will rise up."

9:32   But they failed to understand the word/saying, and they were afraid to ask him.

9:33   And they went/came into Capernaum. And when he was in the house, he asked them, "What were you discussing on the road?"

9:34   But they were silent, for on the road they had been debating among themselves who was greatest.

9:35   And after he sat down, he called the twelve and said to them, "If anyone wishes to be first, he will/must be last of all and servant of all."

9:36   And he took a small child and placed him in their midst, and when he held him in his arms, he said to them (And he took a small child, placed him in their midst, held him in his arms, and said to them),

9:37   "Whoever receives/welcomes one of such little children in my name welcomes me;   and   whoever welcomes me, welcomes not me but the one who sent me."

9:38   John said to him, "Teacher, we saw someone casting   out   demons   in   your   name,   and   we stopped/prevented him, because he is not following us."

9:39   But Jesus said, "Stop forbidding him, for there is no one who will do a miracle in   my   name   who   will also soon be able to curse me/speak evil of me;

9:40   for he who is not against us, is for us.

9:41   For whoever gives you a cup of water to drink in my name because you are of Christ, truly I tell you that he will certainly not lose his reward (by no means lose his reward).

9:42   And whoever causes one of the least of these/these little ones who believe in me to sin, it is better for him if a large millstone is hung around his neck and he is cast/thrown into the sea.

9:43   And if your hand causes you to stumble into sin, cut it off; it is good/better for you to enter into life crippled than having two hands to enter into hell, into the unquenchable[2] fire.

9:44   [omitted]

9:45   And if your foot causes you to stumble into sin, cut it off; for you to enter into life   lame is good/better than having two feet to be cast into hell.

9:46   [omitted]

9:47   And if your eye causes you to stumble into sin, tear it out; for you to enter into the   kingdom of God one-eyed is better than having two eyes to be cast into hell,

9:48   where their worm never dies and the fire is not extinguished/does not go out;

9:49   for all will be restored by fire.[3]

9:50   Salt is good; but if the salt becomes unsalty, with what/how will you restore its flavor?[4] You have salt in yourselves, and you are at peace with one another."

(Imperative: "Have salt in yourselves, and be at peace with one another.")

NOTES

[1]There are three different references here: "When *he* saw *him* the spirit immediately threw *him* into convulsions . . ."

One option: (1) he = Jesus; (2) him/it = spirit; (3) him = the boy; so the translation would be: "When Jesus saw the spirit the spirit immediately threw the boy into convulsions . . ."

Another option: (1) he/it = spirit; (2) him = Jesus; (3) him = the boy; so the translation would be: "When the spirit saw Jesus the spirit immediately threw the boy into convulsions . . ."

[2]Interesting note: The Greek adjective translated "unquenchable" is ἄσβεστος, from which we get our word "asbestos" (a heat-resistant fibrous silicate mineral that can be woven into fabrics, and is used in fire-resistant and insulating materials such as brake linings).

[3] "will be restored" = ἁλισθήσεται from ἁλίζω which means "to salt; to restore flavor to salt." There are two possible interpretations (perhaps both apply):

1. restating the coming judgment in Gehenna;
2. transitioning to discipleship: through sufferings, the disciples are being refined.

[4]Cf. Matthew 5:13: Ὑμεῖς ἐστε τὸ ἅλας τῆς γῆς· ἐὰν δὲ τὸ ἅλας μωρανθῇ, ἐν τίνι ἁλισθήσεται; εἰς οὐδὲν ἰσχύει ἔτι εἰ μὴ βληθὲν ἔξω καταπατεῖσθαι ὑπὸ τῶν ἀνθρώπων ("You are the salt of the earth; but if the salt has lost its saltiness, by what/how will it be restored as salt; it is good for nothing except after being thrown out to be trampled under the feet of people.")

CHAPTER 10

10:1 And after he departed from there, he went/came into the regions of Judea [and] across the Jordan, and again crowds were flocking to him, and as he had been accustomed again he was teaching them.

10:2 And Pharisees, in order to test him, approached and were asking him, "Is it lawful for a man to divorce his wife?"

10:3 So he answered and said to them, "What did Moses command you?"

10:4 They said, "Moses allowed (a man) to write a statement of divorce and to send her away/divorce her."

10:5 So Jesus said to them, "With reference to your stubbornness, Moses wrote this commandment for you.

10:6 But from the beginning of creation, 'he made them male and female;

10:7 for this reason a man will leave his father and mother [and will be united in marriage with his wife],

10:8 and the two will be one flesh; so that they are no longer two but one flesh.'

10:9 Therefore what God has joined together in marriage, let a person not separate."

10:10 And in the house, the disciples were again asking him about this.

10:11 And he said to them, "Whoever divorces his wife and marries another commits adultery with her.

10:12 And if she, after divorcing her husband, marries another, she commits adultery."

10:13   And they were bringing children to him that he might touch them; but the disciples rebuked them.

10:14   But when Jesus saw this, he was indignant and said to them, "Allow the children to come to me, and do not hinder them, for of such kind is the kingdom of God.

10:15   Truly I say to you, whoever does not receive the kingdom of God as a child, will certainly not/by no means enter into it."

10:16   And when he put his arms around them, he blessed them by putting his hands on them.

10:17   And as he set out on a journey, one who had run ahead knelt (before) him and asked him, "Good Teacher, what must I do in order to inherit eternal life?"

10:18   But Jesus said to him, "Why do you call me good? No one is good except the one God.

10:19   You know the commandments, 'You shall not murder,' 'You shall not commit adultery,' 'You shall not steal,' 'You shall not bear false witness,' 'You shall not defraud,' 'Honor your father and mother.'"

10:20   So he said to him, "Teacher, all these things I have kept since/from my youth."

10:21   But Jesus looked straight at him and loved him and said to him, "One thing is lacking for you; go and sell as much as you have and give to the poor, and you will have treasure in heaven, and come follow me."

10:22   But as a result, he was shocked at the word and went away sorrowful, for he had many possessions.

10:23   And when Jesus looked around, he said to his disciples, "How hard it is for the ones who have possessions to enter into the kingdom of God."

10:24   So the disciples were amazed at his words. But Jesus again answered and said to them, "How hard it is to enter the kingdom of God.

10:25   It is easier for a camel to go/pass through the eyes of a needle than (for) a rich person to enter into the kingdom of God."

10:26   But they were even more amazed and said to each other, "Who then is able to be saved?"

10:27   Jesus looked at them and said, "With humans it is impossible but not with God, for all things are possible with God."

10:28   Peter began to say to him, "Look, we have left all things and followed you."

10:29   Jesus said, "Truly I say to you, there is no one who has left house or brothers or sisters or mother or father or children or fields for my sake and for the sake of the kingdom,

10:30   except that he receives one hundredfold now in this time – houses and brothers and sisters and mothers and fathers and fields, with persecutions – and in the age/world that is coming eternal life.

10:31   But many who are the first ones will be last and the last ones will be first."

10:32   They were on the road going up to Jerusalem, and Jesus was going ahead of them, and they were amazed, but those who were following were afraid. And when he took the disciples aside again, he began to tell them/say to them the things about to happen to him,

10:33   that, "Behold! We are going up to Jerusalem, and the Son of man will be delivered over to the chief priests and the scribes, and they will condemn him to death and deliver him over to the Gentiles

10:34   and they will ridicule him and spit on him and whip him and kill (him), and after three days he will rise/come back to life."

10:35   And James and John, the sons of Zebedee, approached him and said to him, "Teacher, we wish that whatever we ask you, you would do for us."

10:36   So he said to them, "What do you wish I would do for you?"

10:37   So they said to him, "Give to us that we might sit in your glory, one at your right and one at your left."

10:38   But Jesus said to them, "You do not know what you are asking. Are you able to drink the cup which I drink, or to be baptized (with) the baptism with which I am (being) baptized?"

10:39   They said to him, "We are able." So, Jesus said to them, "The cup that I drink, you will drink and the baptism with which I am being baptized, you will be baptized,

10:40   but to sit at my right or at my left is not mine to give, but is for those/will be given to those (for whom) it has been prepared."

10:41   And when they heard this, the ten began to be indignant about James and John.

10:42   And when he summoned them, Jesus said to them, "You know that those who seem to rule the Gentiles lord it over them and their great ones tyrannize them.

10:43   But it is not so among you; but whoever wishes to be(come) great among you will be your servant,

10:44   and whoever wishes to be first among you, he will be servant of all;

10:45   for even the Son of man has not come to be served but to serve and to give his life as a means of release for/in place of many."

10:46   And they came/went to Jericho. And as he and his disciples and a large crowd went out from Jericho, the son of Timaeus, Bartimaeus the blind beggar, was sitting beside the road.

10:47   And when he heard that it was Jesus the Nazarene, he began to shout and say, "Son of David Jesus, have mercy on me."

10:48   And many were rebuking him that he might/would be silent; but he cried out all the more, "Son of David, have mercy on me."

10:49   And Jesus stopped and said, "Call him!" And they called the blind man and said to him, "Cheer up! Get up! He is calling you."

10:50   So he threw aside his garment and jumped up and went to Jesus.

10:51   And Jesus answered him and said, "What do you want that I should do for you?" The blind man said to him, "Rabbi, that I should see again/regain my sight."[1]

10:52   And Jesus said to him, "Go, your faith has saved you/made you well." And immediately he saw again/regained his sight, and he was following him on the road.

NOTES

[1]Cf. John 9:11: ἀπεκρίθη ἐκεῖνος, Ὁ ἄνθρωπος ὁ λεγόμενος Ἰησοῦς πηλὸν ἐποίησεν καὶ ἐπέχρισέν μου τοὺς ὀφθαλμοὺς καὶ εἶπέν μοι ὅτι Ὕπαγε εἰς τὸν Σιλωὰμ καὶ νίψαι· ἀπελθὼν οὖν καὶ νιψάμενος ἀνέβλεψα.

ἀνέβλεψα – "look up; regain one's sight; be or become able to see"

It's interesting that Bartimaeus says Ραββουνι, ἵνα ἀναβλέψω and the man in John's gospel says ἀνέβλεψα. Mark and John use the same verb, but John tells us explicitly in 9:1, "As he walked along, he saw a man blind from birth." In Mark's story, Bartimaeus asks to "see again" (not for the first time).

CHAPTER 11

11:1   And when they drew near to Jerusalem to Bethphage and Bethany to the Mount of Olives, he sent two of his disciples

11:2   and said to them, "Go into the village opposite you, and immediately as you enter into it you will a colt tied up upon which no one not yet[1] has ever sat; untie it and bring (it).

11:3   And if anyone says to you, 'Why are you doing this?' say, 'The Lord has need of it, and immediately he sends it back.'"

11:4   And they went out and found a colt tied at the door outside in the street, and they loosened/untied it.

11:5   And some of those who were standing there were saying to them, "What are you doing loosing/untying the colt?"

11:6   And they said to them just as Jesus said; and they allowed them.

11:7   And they took the colt to Jesus, and they laid their garments upon it, and he sat upon it.

11:8   And many of them spread their garments on the road, but others spread leafy branches having cut them from the field.

11:9   And the ones going before and the ones following were shouting/crying out, "Hosanna in the highest! Blessed is the one who comes in the name of the Lord![2]

11:10   Blessed is the coming kingdom of our father David; Hosanna in the highest!"

11:11   And he entered into Jerusalem into the temple; and after he looked around at everything, because the hour was already late, he went out to Bethany with the twelve.

11:12   And on the next day as they departed from Bethany, he was hungry.

11:13   And when he saw from a distance a fig tree which had leaves, he went if perhaps he might find something to eat on it, and when he came to it, he found nothing except leaves; for it was not the season for figs.

11:14   And he answered and said to it, "No longer forever may no one eat fruit from you."[3] And his disciples were hearing.

11:15   And they went into Jerusalem. And when he went into the temple, he began to cast out the sellers and the buyers in the temple, and overturned the tables of the money changers and the chairs of the ones selling doves,

11:16   and he was not permitting that anyone should bring anything through the temple.

11:17   And he was teaching and saying to them, "Is it not written that 'My house shall be called a house of prayer for all the nations?' But you have made it a cave of robbers."

11:18   And the chief priests and the scribes heard (this) and they were seeking how they might destroy/kill him; for they were fearing him, for all the crowd was amazed at his teaching.

11:19   And when it was late in the day/when evening came, they went out from the city.

11:20   And as they were passing by in the morning, they saw the fig tree which had been dried up/withered from its roots.

11:21   And Peter remembered and said to him, "Rabbi, look the fig tree which you cursed is/has withered."

11:22 And Jesus answered and said to him, "Have faith in God/Believe in God.

11:23 Truly I say to you that whoever says to this mountain, 'Be taken up and be cast into the sea,' and does not doubt in his heart but believes that that which he says (will) happen, it will be/happen for him.

11:24 Therefore I say to you, all things whatever you pray (for) and seek/ask for, believe that you have received them, and it will be unto you.

11:25 And whenever you stand praying, forgive if you have anything against anyone, so that also your heavenly Father might forgive you your sins/transgressions."

11:27 And they came again into Jerusalem. And as he was walking around in the temple the chief priests and the scribes and the elders came to him

11:28 and were saying to him, "By what authority are you doing these things? Or who gave you this authority that you might/should do these things?"

11:29 But Jesus said to them, "I will ask you one question, and you answer me, and I will tell you by what authority I do these things.

11:30 Was the baptism of John from heaven or from humans? Answer me."

11:31 And they were debating among themselves and saying, "If we say 'From heaven,' he will say, 'Why therefore did you not believe him?'

11:32 But if we say, 'From people'?" – they were fearing the crowd, for all were thinking that John certainly/truly was a prophet.

11:33 And they answered Jesus and said, "We do not know," and he said to them, "Neither will I tell you by what authority I am doing these things."

NOTES

[1]Double negative – οὐδεὶς οὔπω – "no one not yet."

[2]This is a transliteration of Psalm 118:25-26: "Save us, we beseech you, O LORD! O LORD, we beseech you, give us success! Blessed is the one who comes in the name of the LORD. We bless you from the house of the LORD."

[3]Double negative – Μηκέτι εἰς τὸν αἰῶνα ἐκ σοῦ μηδεὶς καρπὸν φάγοι

CHAPTER 12

12:1   And he began to speak to them in parables, "A man planted a vineyard, and he put a hedge around it and he dug a trough under a wine press, and he built a tower, and he leased it to tenant farmers, and left home on a journey.

12.2   And at the harvest time he sent a slave to the tenant farmers in order that he might receive from the farmers from the fruits of the vineyard.

12.3   And they received him and beat him and sent him away empty-handed.

12.4   And again he sent another slave to them; that one they beat over the head and treated shamefully.

12.5   And he sent another, that one they killed, and (he sent) many others, some of whom they beat but others they killed.

12.6   He had yet one more, a beloved son; he sent him last of all to them and said, 'They will respect my son.'

12.7   But those farmers said to themselves, 'This is the heir; come, let us kill him and we will be the heirs/the property will be ours.'

12.8   And they seized (him) and killed him, and cast him out of the vineyard.

12.9   Therefore, what will the owner of the vineyard do? He will come and destroy the tenant farmers, and give the vineyard to others.

12.10   Have you not read this writing, 'A stone which the builders rejected, this stone has become the main cornerstone/keystone;

12.11   this has come from the Lord, and it is marvelous in our eyes'?"

12.12　And they were seeking to arrest him, but they feared the crowd, for they knew that he told the parable against them. And leaving him they went away.

12.13　And they sent to him some of the Pharisees and Herodians that they might trap him in a word/with a question.

12.14　And they came and said to him, "Teacher, we know that you are true/honest and it is of no concern to you about anyone,[1] for you do not show favoritism (see the face of people), but truly you teach the way of God; is it lawful to pay tax to Caesar or not? Should we pay or should we not pay?"

12.15　But because he perceived their hypocrisy, he said to them, "Why are you testing me? Bring me a denarius that I may see."

12.16　So they brought (it/one). And he said to them, "Of whom is this image and this inscription?" And they said to him, "Of Caesar."

12.17　So Jesus said to them, "The things of Caesar give back to Caesar and the things of God to God." And they were completely amazed at/by him.

12.18　And Sadducees came to him, who say there is no resurrection, and they asked him and said,

12.19　"Teacher, Moses wrote to us that if a brother of someone dies and leaves behind a wife and does not leave a child, that his brother should take the woman/wife and have children for his brother.

12.20　There were seven brothers; and the first took a wife, and when he died, he did not leave behind children;

12.21　and the second took her, and he died without leaving behind children; and the third likewise;

12.22   and the seven did not leave children behind. Last of all, the woman/wife also died.

12.23   In the resurrection, [whenever they should rise] of which of them will she be a wife (whose wife will she be)? For the seven had her as a wife."

12.24   Jesus said to them, "Is this not the reason that you are going astray because you do not know the scriptures nor the power of God?

12.25   For whenever they rise from the dead, they neither marry nor are they given in marriage, but they are as angels in heaven.

12.26   Concerning the dead that are raised, have you not read in the books of Moses how God spoke to him from the bush and said, 'I am the God of Abraham and the God of Isaac and the God of Jacob'?

12.27   He is not God of the dead, but of the living; you have gone much astray (you are much deceived)."

12.28   And when one of the scribes approached and heard them arguing, he saw that he answered them well, and asked him, "Which commandment is first of all?"

12.29   Jesus answered, "The first is, 'Hear, Israel, (the) Lord our God is one Lord (the Lord is one),

12.30   and you shall love the Lord your God from your whole heart and from your whole self and from your whole mind and from your whole strength.'2

12.31   This is a second, 'You will love your neighbor as yourself.' Another commandment is not greater than these. (There is not a commandment greater than these.)"3

12.32   And the scribe said to him, "Well (said), Teacher, you have spoken from truth that he is one and there is not another except him;

12.33   and to love him from the whole heart and from the whole understanding and from the whole strength and to love the neighbor as oneself is greater/more than all of the whole burnt offerings and sacrifices."

12.34   And when Jesus saw [him] that he answered wisely, he said to him, "You are not far from the kingdom of God." And no one any longer dared to question him.[4]

12.35   And Jesus answered and said as he was teaching in the temple, "How do the scribes say that the Christ/Messiah is the son of David?

12.36   David himself said by the Holy Spirit, 'The Lord said to my lord, "Sit (down) at my right (hand), until I place your enemies under your feet."'

12.37   David himself called him Lord, and how is he his son?" And the great crowd was hearing him gladly.

12.38   And in his teaching, he was saying, "Beware of the scribes who like to go around in robes and like greetings in the marketplaces

12.39   and seats of honor in the synagogues and places of honor at the banquets;

12.40   the ones who prey upon/devour the houses of the widows and pray long with a false motive will receive a greater judgment."

12.41   And after he sat down opposite the temple treasury/offering box, he was watching how the crowd was throwing money into the offering box; and many rich people were putting in much;

12.42   and one poor widow came and put in two copper coins, which is about a quadrans.[5]

12.43   And when he had summoned his disciples, he said to them, "Truly I say to you that this poor widow has put in more than all of those who were casting into the box;

12.44   for all of them were putting in from what was left over to them/their wealth, but this one out of her poverty put in all that she had, all her livelihood."

NOTES

[1]Once again, here is the use of the double negative: οὐ μέλει σοι περὶ οὐδενός – "it does not matter to you about no one"

[2]This quotes Deuteronomy 6:5 from the Septuagint (LXX). Compare the Masoretic LXX that says "heart, soul, strength" – δύναμις instead of ἰσχύος..

[3]The order of the Greek words (μείζων τούτων ἄλλη ἐντολὴ οὐκ ἔστιν – "Greater than these another commandment is not" sounds like something Yoda from Star Wars would say.

[4]The use of the double negative – οὐδεὶς οὐκέτι – "no one no longer"

[5]Two copper coins = λεπτά. One λεπτόν was worth ½ quadrans (the smallest Roman coin) or 1/128 denarius. A denarius was a day's wage. A modern eight-hour work day at minimum wage ($7.25) equals $58. 1/128 of $58 = 45¢ -- so an offering of 90¢ -- "all her livelihood!

CHAPTER 13

13:1   And as he was going out from the temple, one of his disciples said to him, "Teacher, see what wonderful stones and what wonderful buildings."

13:2   And Jesus said to him, "Do you see these great buildings? Nothing will be left here, stone upon stone, that will not be destroyed."

13:3   And as he was sitting on the Mount of Olives opposite the temple, Peter and James and John and Andrew were asking him privately,

13:4   "Tell us when will these things be/happen, and what (is the) sign when all these things are going to be completed?"

13:5   So Jesus began to say to them, "Watch out so that no one may lead you astray.

13:6   Many will come in my name and say, 'I am,'[1] and they will lead many astray.

13.7   But whenever you hear of wars and rumors of wars, do not be alarmed; it must be, but the end is not yet.

13:8   For nation will be raised up against nation and kingdom against kingdom, there will be earthquakes in various places, there will be famines; these things are the beginning of the birth-pangs.

13:9   But watch out for yourselves; they will hand you over to the local city councils and in synagogues you will be beaten and you will stand before rulers and kings for my sake as a witness to them.

13:10   And first it is necessary for the gospel to be proclaimed to all the nations.

13:11   And whenever they lead you away in order to hand you over, do not worry ahead of time what you will say, but whatever is given to you in that hour say this, for you are not the ones speaking but the Holy Spirit.

13:12   And brother will hand over brother to death and father child, and children will turn against parents and kill them;

13:13   and you will be hated by all on account of my name. But the one who endures to the end, this one will be saved.

13:14   So whenever you see the object of desecration standing where it is not proper, let the reader understand, then let those in Judea flee into the mountains,

13:15   but let not the one on the rooftop go down nor go in to remove anything/something from his house,

13:16   and the one in the field let him not return to the things left behind to get his garment.

13:17   But how horrible it will be for those who are pregnant and nursing in those days.

13:18   But pray that it might not happen in winter.

13:19   For those days will be (a time of) suffering of such a kind as has not ever happened from the beginning of creation which God created until now and it will never happen again.

13:20   And if the Lord had not cut short the days all flesh would not have been saved. But because of the elect whom he elected he cut short the days.

13:21   And then if anyone says to you, 'Look, here is the Christ, look, there is the Christ,' do not believe him/it.

13:22   For false Christs and false prophets will arise and they will give signs and wonders in order to deceive, if possible, the elect.

13:23 But you watch out; I have warned you (spoken to you before) about all things.

13:24 But in those days after that tribulation

'The sun will be darkened,

and the moon will not give its light,

13:25 and the stars will be falling from the heavens,

and the powers that are in the heavens will be shaken.'

13:26 And then they will see the Son of Man coming in clouds with much power and glory.

13:27 And then he will send (his) angels/messengers and gather his elect from the four winds from the boundary of the earth to the boundary of heaven.

13:28 From the fig tree learn this parable; whenever its branch already has become tender and put out leaves, you know that the summer is near.

13:29 So also you know whenever you see these things happening, you know that it is near to the doors.

13:30 Truly I say to you that this generation will not pass away until all these things happen.

13:31 The heaven(s) and the earth will pass away, but my words will certainly not/never pass away.

13:32 But about that day or hour no one knows, neither the angels in heaven nor the Son, only the Father.

13:33 Beware, be alert; for you do not know when the (appointed) time[2] is.

13:34 (It is) as a man who has left his house and given the authority to his servants, to each his (own) work, and commanded the doorkeeper that he should keep alert.

13:35 Therefore (you) keep watch, for you do not know when the lord of the house is coming, either late in the day or in the middle of the night or before dawn or early morning,

13:36 lest he comes unexpectedly and should find you sleeping.

13:37 And what I say to you, I say to all, Watch!"

NOTES

[1] Ἐγώ εἰμι – "I am" – compare Matthew 24:5 (parallel verse): Ἐγω εἰμι ὁ Χριστός "I am the Christ."

[2] καιρός – an occasion rather than an extent vs. χρόνος – extension or period of time

CHAPTER 14

14:1   It was the Festival of the Passover and the Feast of Unleavened Bread after two days. And the chief priests and the scribes were seeking how to kill him after they arrested him with deceit;

14:2   for they were saying, "Not at the Festival, lest there will be/is a riot among the people."

14:3   And while he was in Bethany in the house of Simon the leper and reclining, a woman came who had an alabaster jar of pure, extremely expensive oil of nard perfume/ointment; and after breaking open the alabaster jar, she poured it over/on his head.

14:4   But there were some[1] who were indignant among themselves/to one another, "For what/why has this destruction/waste of the ointment happened?

14:5   For this ointment was able to be sold/could have been sold for more than three hundred denarii[2] and given to the poor." And they were criticizing her harshly.

14:6   But Jesus said, "Leave her alone; why are you causing trouble for her? She performed a good work for me.

14:7   For you always have the poor with yourselves, and whenever you wish you are able to do good for them, but you do not always have me.

14:8   What she had, she did (what she was able to do, she did); she worked ahead of time to pour perfume on my body for burial preparation.

14:9   For truly I say to you, wherever the gospel is preached in the whole world, also what she has done will be told as a memorial/in memory of her."

14:10   And Judas Iscariot, one of the twelve, went out to the chief priests in order that he might hand him over/betray him to them.

14:11   The ones who heard rejoiced and promised to give him silver/money. And he was seeking when the time was right that he might betray him.

14:12   And on the first day of the Feast of the Unleavened Bread, when they were sacrificing the Passover lamb, his disciples said to him, "When we have gone out, where do you wish us to prepare that we might eat the Passover?"

14:13   So he sent two of his disciples, and said to them, "Go into the city, and a man carrying two jars of water will meet you; follow him,

14:14   and wherever he enters, say to the householder, 'The Teacher says, "Where is my guestroom where I may eat the Passover with my disciples?"'

14:15   And he will show you a large upstairs room furnished and already prepared; and there you prepare for us."

14:16   And the disciples went out and went into the city and found (it) just as he told them, and they prepared the Passover.

14:17   And when it was evening, he came with the twelve.

14:18   And as they were reclining at the table and eating, Jesus said, "Truly I say to you that one of you will betray me, who is eating with me."

14:19   They began to be sad/sorrowful and to say to him one by one, "Is it I?"[3]

14:20   But he said to them, "One of the twelve, the one who is dipping [his hand, the bread] with me into the bowl.

14:21   For the Son of Man goes just as it has been written about him, but woe to that man by/through whom the Son of Man is betrayed; better for him if that man had not been born."

14:22   And while they were eating, when he had taken bread and given thanks, he broke (it) and gave it to them and said, "Take, this is my body."

14:23   And having taken a cup and given thanks, he gave it to them, and all of them drank from it.

14:24   And he said to them, "This is my blood of the covenant which is shed/poured out for many.

14:25   Truly I say to you that I will no longer, never ever[4] drink from the fruit of the vine until that day when I drink (it) anew in the kingdom of God."

14:26   And after they had sung a hymn, they went out to the Mount of Olives.

14:27   And Jesus said to them, "All of you will be led into sin/desert me, because it is written,

'I will strike the shepherd,

and the sheep will be scattered';

14:28   but after I have been raised, I will go ahead of you into Galilee."

14:29   But Peter said to him, "Even if all will desert (you), but not I."

14:30   And Jesus said to him, "Truly I say to you that today by this night before a rooster crows twice, you will deny me three times."

14:31   But he was saying emphatically, "Even if it is necessary for me to die with you, I will never ever (by no means) deny you." And all also were saying likewise.

14:32   And they came to a place called Gethsemane, and he said to his disciples, "Stay/Sit here until/while I pray.'

14:33   And he took along with him Peter and James and John, and he began to be greatly distressed and troubled,

14:34   and he said to them, "My soul is very sad/deeply distressed to the point of death; remain here and keep alert."

14:35   And he went on ahead a little bit and fell on the ground, and he was praying that if it were possible the hour could/would/might pass from him,

14:36   and he said, "Abba Father, all things (are) possible for you; take away this cup from me; but not what I wish/will/want but what you wish/will/want."

14:37   And he came and found them sleeping, and said to Peter, "Simon, are you sleeping? Were you not able to keep watch one hour?

14:38   Keep alert and pray that you might not come into a time of trial; on the one hand the spirit is willing but on the other hand the flesh is weak."

14:39   And again he went away and prayed and said the same word.

14:40   And again when he came, he found them sleeping, for their eyes were very heavy, and they did not know what to answer him.

14:41   And he came a third time and said to them, "Are you sleeping from now on still and resting? It is enough/the account is settled; the hour has come, look the Son of Man is being given over into the hands of the sinners.

14:42   Get up, let us go; look the one who is betraying me has come near."

14:43   And immediately while he was still speaking, Judas, one of the twelve, arrived and with him a crowd with swords and clubs from the chief priests and the scribes and the elders.

14:44   Now the one who was betraying him had given them a sign and said, "Whomever I kiss is he; seize him and lead him away under guard."

14:45   And when he had come, immediately he approached him and said, "Rabbi," and kissed him.

14:46   So they laid their hands on him and seized/arrested him.

14:47   But a certain one of those who were standing by drew his sword and struck the slave of the high priest and cut off his ear.

14:48   And Jesus answered and said to them, "Have you come out as against an insurrectionist in order to arrest me?

14:49   Daily I was with you in the temple teaching and you did not seize me; but in order that the scriptures might be fulfilled . . ."

14:50   And they left him and all fled.

14:51   And a certain young man followed him, dressed in a linen cloth on his naked body, and they seized him.

14:52   But he left behind the linen garment and fled naked.

14:53   And they led Jesus away by force to the high priest, and all of the chief priests and the elders and the scribes assembled together.

14:54   And Peter followed him from a distance as far as inside the courtyard of the high priest, and he was sitting together with the servants and warming himself by the fire.

14:55   But the chief priests and all the Sanhedrin were seeking a witness against Jesus so they might kill him, but they were not finding (one).

14:56   For many were giving false testimony against him, and their testimonies were not alike/in agreement.

14:57   And some rose up and were bearing false witness/testimony against him, saying,

14:58   "We heard him saying 'I will destroy this temple made by human hands and after three days I will build another not made by human hands.'"

14:59   And so in this way their testimony was not even in agreement.

14:60   And the chief priest stood up in the midst and asked Jesus, "Do you not answer anything?[5] Why are they testifying against you?"

14:61   But he was silent and answered nothing.[6] Again the chief priest asked him and said to him, "Are you the Christ, the Son of the Blessed One?"

14:62   So Jesus said, "I am,

and 'You will see the Son of Man

seated at the right hand of power

and coming with the clouds of heaven.'"

14:63   So the chief priest tore his clothes and said, "Why do we still have need of witnesses?

14:64   You heard the blasphemy; what do you think?" And all of them condemned him as deserving of death.

14:65   And some began to spit on him and to cover his face and to strike him, and say to him, "Prophesy," and the guards took him with blows/slaps.

14:66   And while Peter was below in the courtyard, one of the slave-girls of the chief priest came,

14:67   and when she saw Peter warming himself, she looked straight at him and said, "You also were with the Nazarene Jesus."

14:68　But he denied (it) and said, "I neither know nor understand what you are saying/talking about." And he went outside into the forecourt [; and a cock crowed.]

14:69　And when the servant-girl saw him, she began to say again to the bystanders, "This (man) is one of them."

14:70　But again he denied (it). And after a little while again, the bystanders were saying to Peter, "Truly you are one of them, for you are a Galilean."

14:71　But he began to swear/invoke a curse and make an oath, "I do not know this man you are naming/talking about."

14:72　And immediately a cock crowed a second time. And Peter remembered the word which Jesus had said to him, "Before a cock crows twice you will deny me three times"; and he broke down and began to weep.

NOTES

[1]Interestingly, the parallel story in Matthew 26:6-13 identifies "some" as the disciples.

Matthew 26:8 – ἰδόντες δὲ οἱ μαθηταὶ ἠγανάκτησαν λέγοντες, , ,

In John 12:4, it is Judas who complains: λέγει δὲ Ἰούδας ὁ Ἰσκαριώτης εἷς [ἐκ] τῶν μαθητῶν αὐτοῦ, ὁ μέλλων αὐτὸν παραδιδόναι. . .

[2]Three hundred denarii = almost a year's wages. Compare Judas's motive in John 12:6: εἶπεν δὲ τοῦτο οὐχ ὅτι περὶ τῶν πτωχῶν ἔμελεν αὐτῷ ἀλλ᾿ ὅτι κλέπτης ἦν καὶ τὸ γλωσσόκομον ἔχων τὰ βαλλόμενα ἐβάσταζεν.

[3]This form expects (hopes for?) a negative response. Μήτι ἐγώ; "Not I? Surely not I?"

　　"No, not you."

[4]Here is a triple negative! οὐκέτι οὐ μὴ πίω

[5]Another double negative: Οὐκ ἀποκρίνῃ οὐδέν

[6]Again, another double negative! οὐκ ἀπεκρίνατο οὐδέν.

CHAPTER 15

15:1   And as soon as morning came, the chief priests with the elders and the scribes and the whole council, having made a plan and having bound Jesus, led (him) away by force and handed (him) over to Pilate.

15:2   And Pilate asked him, "Are you the king of the Jews?" But Jesus answered him and said, "You say."

15:3   And the chief priests were accusing him of many things.

15:4   So Pilate again asked him and said, "Are you not answering nothing?[1] See how much they are accusing you of."

15:5   But Jesus no more/no longer answered nothing,[2] so that Pilate was amazed.

15:6   At each festival, he (Pilate) released to them one prisoner whom they were requesting.

15:7   The one named Barabbas was bound/imprisoned with the insurrectionists who had committed murder during the rebellion.

15:8   And when the crowd rose up, it began to ask just as he was doing for them.

15:9   Now Pilate answered them and said, "Do you wish that I would release to you the king of the Jews?"

15:10   For he knew that on account of jealousy the chief priests had handed him over.

15:11   But the chief priests incited the crowd so that he might release Barabbas to them instead.

15:12   So Pilate again answered and said to them, "What therefore (do you want) I should do (with him you are calling) the king of the Jews?"

15:13   But again they cried out, "Crucify him!"

15:14   But Pilate said to them, "What evil did he do?" So, they cried out all the more/even louder, "Crucify him!"

15:15   So Pilate, because he wished to satisfy the crowd, released Barabbas to them, and handed Jesus over after he had whipped him, so that he could be crucified.

15:16   Now the soldiers led him away by force into the courtyard, which is the governor's headquarters, and called together the whole cohort.

15:17   And they clothed him in a purple cloak and after weaving a thorny crown they placed (it) on him.

15:18   And they began to greet/salute him, "Greetings, king of the Jews!"

15:19   And they were striking his head with a reed and spitting on him, and when they had knelt down, they were mock-worshiping him.

15:20   And when they had ridiculed him, they stripped him of the purple cloak and dressed him in his own clothes. And they led him out that they might crucify him.

15:21   And they pressed into service a certain passerby who was coming in from the field, Simon a Cyrenian, the father of Alexander and Rufus, to carry his cross.

15:22   And they brought him to the place Golgotha, which is translated "The Place of the Skull."[3]

15:23   And they were giving/offering him wine mixed with myrrh, but he did not take it.

15:24   And they crucified him and were dividing his clothes among themselves by casting lots for them who should/might get what.

15:25 Now it was the third hour when they crucified him.

15:26 And there was an engraved inscription of his charge, "The king of the Jews."

15:27 And with him they crucified two robbers, one on right and one on his left.

15:29 And the passersby were reviling him by shaking their heads and saying, "Ha! The one who was destroying the temple and rebuilding it in three days (you who would destroy the temple and rebuild it in three days),

15:30 save yourself by coming down from the cross (Come down from the cross and save yourself)!"

15:31 Likewise also the chief priests were ridiculing with one another (and) with the scribes and saying, "He saved others, but he is not able to save himself.

15:32 Let the Christ/Messiah, king of Israel come down now from the cross that we might see and believe." And those who had been crucified with him were also insulting him.

15:33 And when it was the sixth hour (12 noon), darkness was over all the land until the ninth hour (3:00 p.m.).

15:34 And at the ninth hour (3:00 p.m.), Jesus cried out in a great voice, "Eloi, eloi, lema sabachthani,"[4] which is translated, "My God, my God, why have you forsaken me/why did you forsake me?"

15:35 And some of those who were standing around, when they heard, said, "Look, he is calling Elijah!"

15:36 But someone ran and also filled a sponge with sour wine, put it on a reed, and gave it to him to drink, and said, "Wait, let us see if Elijah comes to take him down."

15:37 But Jesus, after he gave up a great cry, died.

15:38 And the curtain of the temple was split/ripped in two from top to bottom.

15:39   Now when the centurion who was standing opposite/facing him saw that he had died in this way, he said, "Truly this man was the Son of God."[5]

15:40   Now there were also women watching at a distance, among whom also were Mary Magdalene and Mary the mother of James the younger and Joses, and Salome,

15:41   who were following him and ministering to him when he was in Galilee, and many others who had come up with/traveled with him to Jerusalem.

15:42   And now when evening had come, since it was the Day of Preparation, which is the day before the sabbath,

15:43   when Joseph from Arimathea came, a respected member of the council, who himself was awaiting the kingdom of God, because he was brave, went to Pilate and requested the body of Jesus.

15:44   But Pilate was amazed if already he had died, and when he summoned the centurion, he asked him if he had already died;

15:45   and when he found this out from the centurion, he gave the corpse to Joseph.

15:46   And when he had bought a linen cloth used for burial and taken him down, he wrapped (him) in the cloth and laid him in a tomb which had been hewn from rock, and he rolled a stone against the entrance of the tomb.

15:47   And Mary Magdalene and Mary the mother of Joses were observing/saw where he was laid/placed.

NOTES

[1]Double negative: Οὐκ ἀποκρίνῃ οὐδέν;

[2]Double negative: οὐκέτι οὐδὲν ἀπεκρίθη

[3]The Latin word for skull is calva/calvaria = Calvary.

[4]This is a transliteration of an Aramaic phrase into Koine Greek: Ελωι ελωι λεμα σαβαχθανι. See Psalm 22.

[5] Ἀληθῶς οὗτος ὁ ἄνθρωπος υἱὸς θεοῦ ἦν.

Compare Mark 1:1 – Ἀρχὴ τοῦ εὐαγγελίου Ἰησοῦ Χριστοῦ [υἱοῦ θεοῦ]

CHAPTER 16

16:1   And when the sabbath passed, Mary Magdalene and Mary the mother of James and Salome bought aromatic spices in order that they might go and anoint him.

16:2   And very early in the morning on the first day of the week, when the sun had risen, they went to the tomb.

16:3   And they were saying to themselves, "Who will roll away for us the stone from the entrance to the tomb?"

16:4   And when they looked up, they saw that the stone had been rolled away, for it was exceedingly large.

16:5   And when they went into the tomb, they saw a young man sitting on the right side clothed in a white robe and they were greatly alarmed.

16:6   But he said to them, "Do not be alarmed/amazed; you seek Jesus the Nazarene who has been crucified; he has been raised, he is not here; see the place where they laid/placed him.

16:7   But go, say to his disciples and to Peter that he is going ahead of you into Galilee; there you will see him, just as he said to you."

16:8   And when they went out, they fled from the tomb, for trembling and amazement had them; and they said nothing to no one[1], for they were afraid . . .

NOTES

[1]Double negative καὶ οὐδενὶ οὐδὲν εἶπαν

NARRATIVE VERSION OF

MARK'S STORY

The beginning of the gospel (that is, good news) of Jesus Christ, Son of God. Is this good news *about* Jesus Christ, the good news Jesus Christ ***brought and is***, or both? You'll have to decide . . .

The Lord God said it through Isaiah a long time ago, "Look, I am sending my messenger before you, who will get the way ready; a voice cries out in the wilderness, 'Prepare the way of the Lord, make his paths straight.'"

John the baptizer showed up in the wilderness. He was preaching about a baptism that depended on repentance and accepting forgiveness for your sins. It seems everybody went out to the wilderness – people from all over Judea and the whole city of Jerusalem. They confessed their sins and John baptized them in the Jordan River.

John reminded people of Elijah, another prophet in the wilderness. John looked like a prophet, talked like a prophet, and acted like a prophet. He wore a camel-hair garment tied up with a leather belt and lived off the land, eating locusts and wild honey. John knew his place and his role in God's drama. He told the crowds who flocked to him, "Someone is coming after me who is stronger. In fact, I'm not even worthy to stoop down and untie the straps of his sandals. I'm baptizing you with the water of the Jordan River. That one will baptize you with the Holy Spirit."

Well, it just so happened that Jesus also went out into the wilderness. He was from the little town of Nazareth in Galilee, to the northwest of the Jordan River. Just like everybody else, Jesus was baptized by John in the river. But, unlike everybody else, immediately when Jesus was coming up out of the water, he saw heaven ripped open and God's Spirit coming down on him like a dove. And, as if that wasn't interesting enough, Jesus also heard a heavenly voice say to him, "You are the Son I love. I am very pleased with you." (Dear Reader, remember what I told you about this Jesus at the beginning of the story? Keep that in mind!)

Without further ado, that same Spirit compelled Jesus to go out into a deserted place. He was out there for forty days and Satan was tempting and testing him the entire time. Jesus wasn't completely on his own, however. The wild animals were with him and the angels were taking care of him.

John was arrested. After that happened, Jesus went back north to Galilee so he could preach the good news of and about God. His inaugural address was straightforward, "The time is right. God's kingdom is here. Y'all repent and y'all believe in the good news."

One day when Jesus was walking alongside the Sea of Galilee, he saw two fishermen, brothers named Simon and Andrew. They were tossing their nets into the sea. Jesus said to them, "Follow me, and I will make you fishers of people." There and then Simon and Andrew left their fishing nets and went after Jesus. A little further on, Jesus noticed two more fishermen, brothers named James and John. Their father was Zebedee. They were mending their nets in their boat. Right away Jesus called them. They left Zebedee and the hired help in the boat and followed him.

They traveled to Capernaum, which is on the north shore of the Sea of Galilee. Without delay, Jesus went into the synagogue on the sabbath and was teaching. Those who heard him were amazed, because he had first-hand knowledge and authority, not at all like their religious leaders the scribes. Before you knew it, a man with an unclean spirit was there in the synagogue with them. He cried out, "What business do you have with us, Jesus Nazarene? Are you going to destroy us? I know who you are, the holy one of God!" (Isn't it interesting that this knowledge of who Jesus is, is shared by God, the demons, Jesus, and you, and no one else at this point?) But Jesus ordered him, "Shut up! Leave him!" The unclean spirit convulsed the man, cried out in a loud voice, and left him. Everybody was astounded. They were talking among themselves and wondering, "What is this? A new authoritative teaching. He commands and the unclean spirits obey him." In a New York minute, the word got out about him throughout the whole Galilean region.

They left the synagogue and straightaway went to the house of Simon and Andrew. James and John were with them. Simon's mother-in-law was down with a fever. They told him about her, so Jesus went in where she was, took her by the hand, and helped her get up. Her fever broke and left her. She started to wait on them. At sundown, the neighbors were bringing all of the sick folks and those who were demon-possessed. It was as if everybody in the city were there. Jesus healed people of all kinds of illnesses and exorcised lots of demons. Interestingly, Jesus wouldn't let the demons talk, because they knew who he was.

The next morning, while it was still dark, Jesus got up and went out to a lonely place and was praying. Simon and the rest of them went searching for him. When they finally found him, they told him, "Everybody is looking for you." But Jesus said, "C'mon, let's get out of here and head into some other towns. I'll preach there. After all, that's why I have come." And so, he went throughout Galilee, preaching in their synagogues and casting out demons.

A leper came to Jesus, begged him, knelt before him, and said, "If you want to make me clean, you can." Since Jesus had compassion for this man, he stretched out his hand, touched him, and said, "I want to. Be cleansed!" Instantaneously, the leprosy left the man and he was cleansed. Not only was he physically healed, he was also welcomed back into the community. He would no longer have to live on the fringes of society. As Jesus was sending him away, he strongly commanded him, "Don't tell anybody anything about this. Do your duty. Go to the priest and make an offering for your cleansing, just as Moses commanded and as a testimony." But you know what? That guy couldn't help but go out and tell everybody about what had happened. As a result, Jesus could no longer go into a city in plain view. And even though he withdrew to deserted places, people were still coming to him from all directions.

From there Jesus went again to Capernaum. Word got out that he was there and people figured out where the house was where he was staying. So many people flocked to that house, there was hardly room for another person to squeeze in the house or gather at the door. And Jesus was teaching the Word to them.

Then a most unusual thing happened. Four men brought a paralytic on a stretcher to the house but, because the crowd was so large, they climbed up on the roof and started removing the roof tiles and digging through the earthen roof. When they finally made a hole large enough, they lowered the lame man down through the hole. When Jesus saw their faith, he said to the paralytic, "My child, your sins are forgiven."

Some of the religious leaders known as scribes were sitting there. They were wondering, "Why is this guy saying this? Blasphemy! No one can forgive sins except the one true God!"

Instantly Jesus sensed in his spirit that the scribes were wondering about what he had said to the paralytic, so he asked them, "Why are you questioning in your hearts? Let me ask you something. Is it easier to say 'Your sins are forgiven' or 'Get up, pick up your mat, and walk'? But just so you know that the Son of Man has the authority here on earth to forgive sins" – at that point, Jesus turned to the healed man and said, "I tell you, get up, pick up your mat, and go to your house." At once he got up, picked up his mat, and right there in front of everyone, he walked away. Everybody was amazed! They glorified God and said, "We've never seen anything like this!"

Again, Jesus went out to the sea. A crowd was gathered around him and he taught them. As he walked by, he saw a man named Levi, who was the son of Alphaeus, sitting in the tax office. Jesus said, "Follow me," and so Levi got up and followed him.

Now, it just so happened that one day, Jesus was eating and enjoying table fellowship with a lot of tax collectors and sinners and his disciples. By this time, many people were following Jesus. Once again, the scribes of the Pharisees (who were lay religious leaders) saw Jesus eating with the tax collectors and sinners and asked the disciples, "Why does he eat with these people, sinners and tax collectors?" Jesus overheard their question and said to them, "If you're well, you don't need a doctor; only when you're sick. I haven't come to call righteous people, but sinners."

John's disciples and the Pharisees were fasting, and they noticed that Jesus's disciples weren't. So, they asked Jesus about it. Jesus replied, "The friends of the groom don't fast at a wedding, do they? As long as the groom is with them, they're not going to fast. But one day, they won't have the groom with them anymore; that's when they'll fast. If you need to fix a tear in an old shirt, you don't sew a new piece of cloth on it. Do that, and the new piece will rip away from the old and the tear will only be worse. In the same way, no one puts new wine into old skins. If you do, as the new wine ferments, it will bust the old skins and you end up losing the wine and the skins. New wine goes into new skins."

One sabbath, Jesus and his disciples were walking through a grainfield. The disciples plucked the heads of grain as they made their way through the field. The Pharisees asked Jesus, "Look, here, why are your disciples doing what is not allowed on the sabbath?" Jesus answered, "Don't you remember what David and his men did when they were hungry? He went into God's house when Abiathar was high priest and ate the bread that had been offered to God, even though no one was allowed to eat it except the high priest. Why, David even shared it with his men." He told them, "The sabbath was made for our sake; we weren't made to serve the sabbath. So, the Son of Man is Lord – even of the sabbath!"

One day, Jesus was in a synagogue. A man there had a withered hand. The religious leaders were keeping an eye on Jesus, to see if he would heal the man on the sabbath. If he did, they could charge him with violating the law. Jesus said to the man with the withered hand, "Come here and stand in the middle of us." Then he asked the religious leaders, "Is it lawful to do good on the sabbath or to do evil, to save life or to kill?" But none of the leaders said anything. Jesus looked at them. He was angry because of their stubbornness and hard hearts. He told the man, "Stretch out your hand." When the man stretched out his hand, it was healed and made right. The Pharisees left, and in no time, they hatched a plan to kill Jesus.

From there, Jesus and his disciples again went to the sea. The word had gotten out about the things Jesus was doing, and crowds followed him from Galilee. Also, lots of people showed up from Judea, Jerusalem, Idumea, beyond the Jordan, and from around Tyre and Sidon. Afraid that the crowd might crush him, Jesus told his disciples to get a boat ready for him. The more he healed people, the more they crowded him and tried to touch him. Every time Jesus came up against the evil spirits, they recognized him, fell down before him, and cried out, "You are the Son of God!" (Remember, dear reader, at this point you share this insider information with the demons!) Jesus forcefully commanded the demons not to make known his identity as the Son of God.

Jesus went up on the mountain and called those he wanted to join him. When they arrived, he appointed twelve of them to be with him. He was going to send them out to preach (so he called them apostles or "sent ones") and to cast out demons. These are the twelve he appointed: Simon whom he called Peter; James the son of Zebedee and his brother John (Jesus nicknamed them Boanerges, Sons of Thunder!);

Andrew; Philip; Bartholomew; Matthew; Thomas; James the son of Alphaeus; Thaddeus; Simon the Cananaean; and Judas Iscariot who betrayed him to death.

Jesus went to a house. Once again, the crowd was so large, Jesus and his disciples couldn't even eat bread. When Jesus's family heard he was there, they went to get him, because they thought he was out of his mind. Some of the scribes who had come down from Jerusalem said, "He has Beelzebul. That's how he casts out demons – by the power of the ruler of the demons!" Jesus gathered them and spoke to them in parables. "How can Satan cast out Satan? A kingdom at odds with itself cannot long stand, and the same is true of a divided house. So, if Satan works against himself and is divided, then it follows that Satan will not last long. Nobody breaks into a strong man's house and begins to plunder without first binding the strong man. Only then will the burglar begin to plunder the house. Truly I tell you, all of the sins and blasphemies that people commit will be forgiven; but if anyone blasphemes against the Holy Spirit, that person will never be forgiven and will be guilty of an eternal sin." --- Jesus said all of this because the religious leaders were saying, "He has an unclean spirit."

Jesus's mother and brothers went to the house where he was staying, stood outside, and called for him. The people who were sitting around Jesus inside told him, "Your mother, brothers, and sisters are outside looking for you." Jesus asked, "Who are my mother and my brothers?" Then he looked at all of those who were sitting in the circle with him and said, "Look, here are my mother and brothers. Whoever does the will of God is my brother and sister and mother."

Another time he started teaching beside the sea. There was such a big crowd gathered around him that he got into a boat and put out in the water, while the crowd stayed on the land. He was teaching them many things by telling parables, such as, "Listen! A sower went out to sow. While he was scattering seeds, some fell beside the road. The birds flew down and ate the seeds. Other seeds fell on rocky ground where there wasn't much depth of soil. They quickly sprouted because the soil was thin. Still other seeds fell among the thornbushes, which grew up and choke out the plants. They didn't produce any fruit. But some seeds fell in good soil and bore fruit. They grew up, and when they reached maturity they bore fruit, thirty, sixty, and in one case even a hundredfold." Jesus said, "Make sure you listen!"

When Jesus was alone with the disciples and some others, they asked him about the parables. He told them, "You have been given the mystery of the kingdom of God. But all things are in parables to those who are on the outside. This is just as it was said before, 'Even though they see, they will see and not know, and even though they hear, they will hear but not understand. Otherwise, they might turn and be forgiven.'"

He asked them, "Don't you know this parable? How will you understand all the parables? The sower is sowing the Word. Now there are some who are beside the road. When they hear, in the blink of an eye Satan comes and snatches away the Word that was sown among them. The ones sown on rocky ground are those who hear the Word with joy. But, because they don't have deep roots in themselves, when any trouble or hard times come, in a flash they fall away. The ones sown in the thornbushes are those who hear the Word, but daily anxieties and the deception of being rich creep in and choke out the Word, and their lives don't bear any fruit. But the ones who are sown on the good soil hear the Word, receive it, and bear fruit, thirty, sixty, and a hundredfold."

He told them another parable. "Do you bring a lamp into a room and hide it under a basket or shove it under the bed? Don't you put it on the lampstand? Everything that is hidden will be revealed, and everything that is stored away will be brought out into the open. If you have ears, you'd better listen up!"

He told them, "Pay attention to what you hear. You will be judged and measured by the same criteria you use to judge and measure others. More will be given to those who already have; but those who don't have will have what little they do have taken away."

Jesus said, "So, the kingdom of God is like a man who plants grass seed in his yard. He goes to sleep and wakes up, day in and day out. Meanwhile, the grass grows, but he doesn't know how. The earth produces of itself like this: first there is a stalk; then a head of grain appears. When that head matures, then the full grain appears. When the crop is ripe and ready, he promptly sends for the sickle. It's harvest time!"

He said, "How can we describe the kingdom of God? What parable would do it justice? Think about a mustard seed. It's the smallest of all seeds. But, when you sow it upon the earth, it grows up into the largest of all garden plants. Why, its branches are so big the wild birds of the air can nest in its shade."

Jesus used to talk to them with many such parables, as much as they were able to hear. In fact, he never spoke without telling parables. However, privately he explained everything to his disciples.

When evening came that day, Jesus said to them, "Let's cross over to the other side." So, they left the crowd and took Jesus just as he was. They got into a boat and there were other boats with them. A great windstorm blew up, the waves were beating against the boat, and the boat was filling up with water. Now, Jesus was asleep on a cushion in the back of the boat. They woke him up and said, "Teacher, don't you care that we're perishing?" After they woke him up, he commanded the wind and said to the sea, "Calm down! Shut up!" The wind stopped and there was a great calm. Then Jesus asked them, "Why are you afraid? Don't you have faith yet?" They were terrified and said to each other, "Who is this guy? Even the wind and the sea obey him."

They went to the other side of the sea into the region of the Gerasenes. Straight away, when Jesus was getting out of the boat, a man with an unclean spirit confronted him. This guy lived among the tombs. Time and again, he was bound with foot chains and shackles, but he always broke free. Nobody could restrain him. All night and day, he would roam among the graves and in the mountains and cry out and bruise himself with rocks. While he was still a ways off, he saw Jesus. He ran to Jesus, fell down before him, and worshiped him. The man screamed at the top of his lungs, "What business do you and I have, Jesus Son of the Most High God? I beg you, don't torment me!" It's almost as if the demon were trying to gain the upper hand, because Jesus was telling him, "Unclean spirit, come out of him!" Jesus asked him, "What is your name?" and he answered, "Legion, because we are many!" He begged Jesus over and over not to banish them.

There was a large herd of pigs grazing near the mountain. The demon begged Jesus to send them into the pigs, so he allowed it. The unclean spirits left the man and entered the pigs. The pigs – about 2,000 of them – rushed down the steep embankment into the sea and drowned. The pig herders ran away and told everybody what Jesus had done and they all went to see what had happened.

When they got to Jesus, they also saw the man who had been demon-possessed with Legion. Lo and behold, he was sitting there, completely dressed and in his right mind! And guess what? They were afraid! The people who were there when it happened also told the late-comers about the pigs. They begged Jesus to get out of town. As Jesus was getting in the boat to do just that, the man who had been demon-possessed begged to go with him. But Jesus told him no. Instead, he said, "Go home and tell your family and neighbors how much the Lord has done for you and how he has shown you kindness." So, he did just that. He went all around the area of the Decapolis (the Ten Cities) and shared how much Jesus had done for him. Everybody was amazed!

When Jesus got to the other side of the sea, a large crowd flocked to him. One of the synagogue leaders, a man named Jairus, came, saw Jesus, fell down before him, and begged him from his heart, "My little girl is sick and dying! Come, lay your hands on her so she can be healed and live!" So, Jesus went with him. A great crowd followed him and pressed in on him from all sides.

There was a woman who had suffered from a bleeding disorder for twelve years. She had spent all of her money on many doctors, but never got better. When she heard about Jesus, she joined the throng, made her way up to him from behind, and touched his robe. She had told herself (and hoped), "If I can just touch his robe, I'll be made well." In nothing flat, her bleeding stopped and she could feel in her body that she had been cured. Quick as a wink, Jesus sensed that power had gone out from him, so he turned and asked, "Who touched my clothes?" But his disciples said, "You see this huge crowd all around you, and yet you're wondering who touched you?" Still, Jesus was looking around to see who had touched him. The woman knew what had happened to her and, even though she was shaking with fear, fell down at Jesus's feet and told him the truth. Jesus said to her, "Daughter, your faith has healed and saved you. Go in peace. Your illness has been cured."

Even while Jesus was still speaking to the woman, some people came out of the leader's house and told him, "Your daughter died. Don't trouble the teacher anymore." But Jesus overheard the message and said to the synagogue leader, "Don't be afraid! Believe!" Jesus didn't let anyone go with him except Peter and the two brothers, James and John. When they went into the leader's house, they saw chaos and heard much weeping and wailing. Jesus said to them, "Why are you so riled up and weeping? The child isn't dead. She's sleeping." And they laughed at him. But Jesus threw all of them out of the house and took the father, mother, and Peter, James, and John in where the little girl was. He took her hand in his and said to her in his native Aramaic language, "Talitha cum," which means something like, "Sweetie, get up!" All of a sudden, she got up and started to walk around. She was twelve years old. At that instant, they were completely amazed. Jesus ordered them sternly not to tell anyone about what had happened. He also told them to give her something to eat.

Jesus went out from there and his disciples were following him to his hometown. When the sabbath came and he was teaching in the synagogue, many heard him, were amazed, and said, "Where did he get all of this teaching? What kind of wisdom is this? What about these miracles he's doing? Isn't his father the carpenter? He's Mary's son and the brother of James and Judas and Simon, isn't he? And aren't his sisters here among us?" They had their doubts about him, even rejecting him. Jesus said to them, "Only in his hometown and among his family and in his own house is a prophet dishonored." Other than laying his hands on a few sick people and healing them, he couldn't do any miracles there. He was amazed at their unbelief.

He summoned the twelve disciples, gave them authority over the unclean spirits, and sent them out two-by-two. He ordered them to pack light – just a bag, sandals, and one cloak, not even bread, a staff, or a money belt. His instructions were, "Whenever you enter a house, stay there until it's time to move on. If someone doesn't receive you or listen to you, walk away and shake the dust off of your feet as a witness against them." They went out, proclaimed repentance, cast out demons, anointed many sick people with oil, and healed them.

Now, King Herod heard about all of this, because Jesus's name was getting to be well known. People were saying,

"That John who was baptizing must have been raised from the dead. That's how and why all these miracles are being done." But other people were saying, "It's Elijah." Still others claimed he was one of the prophets. When Herod heard these things about Jesus, he said, "It's John whose head I had cut off. He's been raised."

You see, Herod himself had sent for John, only to have him arrested and thrown into prison. It all stemmed from Herod having married his sister-in-law Herodias, his brother Philip's wife. John had told Herod, "It's against the law for you to marry your brother's wife." No surprise, Herodias was hostile toward John. She wanted to kill him, but couldn't because Herod was afraid of John. He knew John was a righteous man, a holy man, so he protected him. Even though Herod was greatly disturbed when he listened to John's preaching, still he was glad to hear him.

Things fell into place for Herodias when Herod hosted a birthday bash for himself. The guest list included members of the upper-class, high-ranking officials, and the movers and shakers in Galilee. At one point, his daughter by Herodias came in and danced, which pleased everyone. The king told her, "Whatever you want, I'll give it to you." Then he upped the ante, "Whatever you want is yours. Why, I'll give you half of my kingdom!" The girl went to her mother and said, "What should I ask for?" and her mother said, "The head of John the Baptist." Without hesitation, the girl hurried back to the king and announced, "I want you to give me John the Baptist's head, right now!" Well, even though the king was sad, he really had no choice because he had sworn to her before all of his important guests. He didn't want to tell her no. With all speed, the king ordered the executioner to bring John's head. So he went to the prison, decapitated him, carried John's head on a platter, and gave it to the girl, and the little girl gave it to her mother. When John's disciples heard what had happened, they went and got his corpse and buried it.

The apostles met with Jesus and told him everything they had done and taught. He said, "C'mon, let's get away by ourselves to a little out of the way place so you guys can rest." There were so many people coming and going they didn't even have time to eat. So, they went by boat to a deserted place. But people saw them leaving and recognized them. So, from cities all around the area, people hurried to that place and beat the disciples and Jesus there.

When Jesus got out of the boat, he saw a really big crowd and he felt sorry for them. They were like sheep without a shepherd. He began to teach them many things. Late in the day, his disciples came to him and said, "This is a lonely place and it's late. Tell them to leave so they can go into the villages and find themselves something to eat." But he asked them, "How much bread do you have? Go and find out." When they found out, they told him, "Five loaves and two fish." In response, Jesus said, "You give them something to eat." They said, "What?! We're supposed to go and spend two-thirds of a year's salary to buy some bread and give it to them?" Jesus commanded them to organize the crowd into groups in the green grass. The people sat down in groups of fifty and one hundred. Jesus took the five loaves and the two fish and looked up into heaven. Then he said a blessing over the food, tore the loaves into pieces, and gave the pieces to the disciples so they in turn could give the bread to the people. Jesus also divided the two fish among all of them. Everybody ate until they were satisfied. They gathered up twelve baskets of leftover fish and bread. The crowd was estimated to be 5,000 men. And very quickly he put his disciples in a boat and sent them on ahead of him to Bethsaida on the other side. He stayed behind to send the crowd away. After he told them goodbye, he went to the mountain to pray.

When evening came, the boat was out in the middle of the sea and Jesus was alone on the land. He saw the disciples straining at the oars because the wind was blowing against them. Some time between 3:00 and 6:00 a.m., he walked out on the water to them. He wanted to pass them by. But when they saw him walking on water, they thought he was a ghost, so they cried out. They all saw him and were terrified. But pronto he told them, "Take heart! It's me. Don't be afraid!" When he approached them in the boat, the wind ceased and they were absolutely dumbfounded. They didn't understand about the loaves of bread and their hearts were stubborn.

When they crossed over to the land, they tied up at Gennesaret. When they got out of the boat, lickety-split people recognized him. They hurried all around that territory and brought sick people on stretchers to him. Whenever he went into a village or city, people put the sick in the marketplaces and begged him to let them touch at least the hem of his garment. Whoever touched him was healed and saved.

The Pharisees and some of the scribes who had come from Jerusalem gathered around him. They noticed that some of Jesus's disciples were eating without first washing their hands according to the ritual laws. You see, the Pharisees and all the rest of the Jews are very observant of the traditions of the elders so they are very careful to do things such as washing their hands carefully in the prescribed manner before they eat and not eating whatever they buy from the marketplace without washing first. They also have many other rituals, such as washing cups, pots, copper vessels, and beds.

Anyway, when they noticed what his disciples were doing, the Pharisees and scribes asked Jesus, "Why don't your disciples live according to the traditions of the elders? Why do they eat bread without first washing their hands?" Jesus answered, "You know what? Isaiah the prophet was right about y'all when he wrote, 'These people honor me with their lips, but their heart is far from me. Their worship is in vain because they teach human doctrines and rules.' You put human traditions ahead of God's commandments." He repeated himself, "You invalidate God's commandment in order to establish your own tradition. Remember what Moses said? 'Honor your father and your mother,' and 'Whoever speaks evil of or curses father or mother should be put to death.' But listen to what you say – 'Corban! Gift!' You twist the law to your own benefit and use what is meant to help father and mother for your own gain. When you do this, you cancel out God's Word. You hand down this and many other human traditions."

Jesus once again called the crowd to him and said, "Everybody, listen up! Nothing that goes into a person's body can defile it. Instead, the things that come out defile. If you've got ears, listen and understand!" When Jesus went into the house to get away from the crowd, his disciples asked him about the parable. He said, "What, you don't understand either? Don't you get that anything and everything that goes into a person can't defile the person? Why? Because it doesn't go into the human heart but into the stomach and then right into the latrine" (notice how Jesus here declares all things ritually clean). In other words, Jesus was saying, "It's what goes out of the heart – evil thoughts, sexual immorality, theft, murder, adultery, coveting, wickedness, deceit, sensuality, envy, blasphemy, arrogance, foolishness – these kinds of things come from the heart and defile a person."

Jesus left there and went into the region of Tyre. He found a house to stay in. He tried to avoid the crowds, but he couldn't escape notice. ASAP a woman whose daughter had an unclean spirit heard he was in town. She came to him and fell down at his feet. Now, you need to understand, reader, this woman was a Gentile, a Greek, a Syrophoenician by race. She asked Jesus if he would cast out the demon from her daughter. Jesus said to her, "Let the children be fed first. It's just not right and good to take bread out of the mouths of children and throw it to the dogs." The woman answered him, "You're right, sir, but even the little dogs under the table eat the crumbs that the little children drop." Jesus said, "Because of what you just said, go. The demon has left your daughter." When the woman got home, she found her little girl lying in her bed and the demon long gone.

Jesus left the region of Tyre and went through Sidon to the Sea of Galilee and on into the region of the Decapolis (which means "Ten Cities"). The folks there brought a deaf and mute man to Jesus and begged him to lay hands on him. Jesus took the man aside privately to heal him. Here's how he did it: he put his fingers in the man's ears and then he spat and touched it to the man's tongue. Then Jesus looked up to heaven, groaned, and said to the man, "Ephatha!" That means, "Be opened!" And, in a split second, the man's tongue was loosed and he began to speak correctly. Now, Jesus ordered everybody there not to tell anybody about what they had seen. But, wouldn't you know it, the more he told them not to tell, the more they told it! The onlookers were just absolutely amazed and dumbfounded by what they had seen. They said, "He's done everything well. He even makes deaf people hear and mute people talk."

Around that time, Jesus was with a great crowd. It turns out the people didn't have anything to eat. So, Jesus called his disciples together and said to them, "I really feel sorry for these people. Here they've already been with me for three days and now they don't have anything to eat. If I send them home hungry, they're going to faint on the road. And some of them have come from a long way off." His disciples asked him, "How will anybody be able to feed them bread in this forsaken, deserted place?" Jesus asked them, "How many loaves of bread do you have?" They said, "Seven." After he told everybody in the crowd to sit down on the ground, Jesus took the seven loaves, gave thanks, broke them, and gave them to his disciples so they could hand out the bread to the people. They also had a few small fish which Jesus blessed and said to give out, also. Everybody ate until they were full. There were seven baskets of abundant leftovers. Now, there were about 4,000 men there that day (and that probably doesn't even count women and children). Then Jesus sent them away.

Directly, after he got into the boat with his disciples, he went into the region of Dalmanutha. The Pharisees went out and started arguing with him. They wanted him to give them a sign from heaven. In reality, they were testing him. Jesus groaned deep in his spirit and said, "Why does this generation seek a sign? Why, I tell you, even if a sign is given to this generation . . ." Jesus left the thought hanging; in other words, "This is NOT going to happen!"

Jesus left them, got in the boat, and went over to the other side. They forgot to take enough bread with them. They only had one loaf. And Jesus was strongly advising them, "Watch out, understand, and beware of the yeast of the Pharisees and of Herod." Now, the disciples thought he was talking about bread, so they were talking among themselves about the fact that they didn't have any bread. Jesus knew that's what they were talking about, so he asked them, "Why are y'all talking about not having any bread? Do you still not understand? Are your hearts so stubborn? You have eyes but you don't see. You have ears but you do not hear and understand. Don't you remember when I broke the five loaves for the 5,000? How many baskets of leftovers did we have?" They said, "Twelve." And he said, "And what about when I broke the seven loaves for the 4,000, how many baskets of leftovers did you gather up?" They said, "Seven." And Jesus asked, "Do you still not understand?"

When they got to Bethsaida, some people brought a blind man to him and begged him to touch him. Jesus took the man by the hand and led him out of the village. He spat on the man's eyes, put his hands on him, and asked, "What do you see? Anything?" The man regained his sight somewhat and said, "I see people walking around, but they look like trees." Jesus put his hands on the man's eyes a second time and his sight was restored. He was cured and saw everything clearly. Jesus sent him home with these instructions, "Don't go into the village."

Jesus and his disciples went into the villages of Caesarea Philippi. Along the way he asked them, "What are people saying about me? Who do they think I am?" They replied, "Some say you're John the Baptist, while others think you're Elijah or one of the prophets.? Jesus asked them, "How about all of you? Who do you think I am?" Peter answered, "You're the Christ!" (which means the Anointed One or the Messiah). Jesus told them not to talk about him in this way with anyone. Then Jesus began to teach them that it would be necessary for the Son of Man to suffer many things, be rejected by the elders and the high priest and the scribes, be killed, and rise again after three days. He said this quite openly and plainly. Peter took him aside and began to rebuke him. But Jesus turned, saw his disciples, and then he rebuked Peter, "Get behind me, Satan! You're not thinking from God's perspective. Your thoughts are human thoughts." Then he summoned the crowd to gather with his disciples and said, "Let those who want to follow after me take up their crosses and follow me. Those who want to save their lives will only lose them. But those who lose their lives on account of me and the gospel will save their lives. What profit does a person get from gaining the whole world but losing her life? What can a person give up in exchange for his life? Whoever is ashamed of me and my words in this unfaithful and sinful generation, the Son of Man will also be ashamed of that person whenever he comes in the Father's glory with his holy angels." And he said to them, "Trust me, some of you standing here will not die before you see God's kingdom coming with power."

Six days later, Jesus privately took Peter, James, and John to a high mountain where he was transformed. His clothes became whiter than any earthly bleach could whiten them. Elijah and Moses appeared to them and were talking with

Jesus. Not knowing what he was talking about because he and the other disciples were terrified, Peter said, "Rabbi, it's a good thing we're up here. Let's pitch three tents, one for you, one for Moses, and one for Elijah." A cloud surrounded them and voice out of the cloud said, "This is my beloved Son. Listen to him." And in a jiffy, when they looked around, they realized they were alone with Jesus.

As they were coming down from the mountaintop, Jesus ordered them not to tell anyone what they had seen, until the Son of Man might rise from the dead. So, they kept mum on the subject, but at the same time they wondered what this "rising from the dead" business might mean. On the way down, they asked Jesus, "Why do the scribes say that it was necessary for Elijah to come first?" Jesus answered, "I tell you the truth, Elijah has come first and restored all things. How is it written about the Son of Man, that he should suffer many things and be rejected? Hear me out – Elijah has come, and they did whatever they wanted to him, just as it had been written about him."

When they got to the bottom of the mountain, they saw a large crowd surrounding the disciples and scribes arguing with them. At the drop of a hat, the whole crowd saw Jesus, was amazed, and ran up and greeted him. Jesus asked them, "What are you debating with them?" Somebody in the crowd called out, "Teacher, I brought my son to you because he has a spirit that keeps him from talking. When the spirit attacks, it throws my boy to the ground and he foams at the mouth, grinds his teeth, and becomes stiff as a board. I asked your disciples to cast it out, but they couldn't do it." Jesus said, "You faithless generation! How long do I have to be with you and put up with you? Bring the boy to me." So, they brought the boy to Jesus. When the spirit saw Jesus, he pell-mell threw the boy into convulsions. The boy fell to the ground and rolled around and foamed at the mouth. Jesus asked the boy's father, "How long has he been like this?" "Since he was a child," said the father. "Many times the spirit has thrown him into fire and water and tried to kill him. If you can do something, help us and have compassion on us!" Jesus responded, "Now about 'If you can . . .' All things are possible for the one who believes." In no time at all the father of the child cried out, "I believe! Help my unbelief!" When Jesus saw the crowd hurrying toward them, he commanded the unclean spirit, "Mute and deaf spirit, I command you to come out of him. You will no longer be able to enter into him." After the spirit cried out and threw the boy into hard convulsions, it came out. The boy looked as if he were dead. In fact, many of the people were saying, "He's dead." But Jesus took his hand and raised him up, and the boy stood up. After it was all over and he had gone into a house, Jesus's disciples asked him in private, "Why couldn't we cast it out?" He told them, "This kind can't come out except by prayer."

They went out from there and passed through Galilee. He didn't want anyone to know. On the way he was teaching his disciples, "The Son of Man will be handed over into human hands. They will kill him. Three days after he has been killed, he will rise up." Now, they didn't understand what he was talking about and they were afraid to ask him.

When they arrived in Capernaum and were in the house, Jesus asked them, "What were y'all talking about on the road?" They didn't say anything because they had been debating which of them was the greatest. Jesus sat down and called the twelve of them over. "If you want to be first of all," he explained, "you must be last and servant of all." Then he took a small child, put him in the middle of all of them, held him in his arms, and said, "Whoever welcomes one of these little children in my name, welcomes me. Not only that, whoever welcomes me also welcomes the one who sent me."

John said, "Teacher, we saw someone casting out demons in your name. We stopped him, though, because he is not one of us." But Jesus replied, "Don't keep him from doing that. Anybody who does a miracle in my name won't soon be able to speak evil of me. If you're not against us, you're for us. Listen, whoever gives you a cup of cold water in my name because you are 'from Christ,' believe me, that one by no means will lose his reward. Furthermore, if somebody causes one of these little ones who believe in me to sin, it would be better for him to have a big millstone tied around his neck and to be thrown into the sea. If your hand causes you to sin, cut it off! It's better to enter into life with only one hand than to enter into the unquenchable fire of hell with two hands. If your foot causes you to sin, cut it off! It's better for you to enter life lame than to have two feet and to be cast into hell. And if your eye causes you to sin, pluck it out! It's better for you to enter the kingdom one-eyed than to be cast into hell with two eyes, where the worm never dies and the fire never goes out. For all will be restored by fire. Salt is good; but if salt loses its saltiness, how will you restore its flavor? Have salt in yourselves and be at peace with one another."

After he departed from there, Jesus went into the regions of Judea and across the Jordan. Once again, the crowds flocked to him and as he had been doing in other places, he taught them. Some Pharisees approached him and, in order to test him, asked, "Is it lawful for a man to divorce his wife?" Jesus asked them in return, "What did Moses command you?" They answered, "Moses allowed a man to write out a statement of divorce and to divorce her." Jesus said, "Moses wrote this commandment for you because you're stubborn. From the beginning of creation, God made them male and female. That's why a man will leave his father and mother and be married to his wife, and the two become one flesh. They are no longer two but one flesh. What God joins together in marriage a person shall not separate." When they were back in the house, the disciples asked him about this again. Jesus said, "Whoever divorces his wife and marries another woman commits adultery with her. And if a woman divorces her husband and marries another man, she commits adultery."

People were bringing children to Jesus so he could touch them, but the disciples rebuked them. Jesus was indignant when he saw this and told them, "Let the children come to me. Don't keep them away. The kingdom of God belongs to such as these. I really mean it – if you don't receive the kingdom of God as a child, you'll never enter into it." Then he hugged the children and blessed them by laying his hands on them.

As he set out again on a journey, a man ran ahead and knelt before Jesus and asked, "Good Teacher, what do I have to do in order to inherit eternal life?" Jesus said to him, "Why do you call me good? No one is good except the one God. You know the commandments – 'You shall not murder,' 'You shall not commit adultery,' 'You shall not steal,' 'You shall not bear false witness,' 'You shall not defraud,' 'Honor your father and mother.'" The man said to Jesus, "Teacher, I have kept all of these things since I was a child." Jesus looked him in the eye and said, "One thing is missing. Sell everything you have and give the money to the poor. Then you will have treasure in heaven. Come, follow me." But the man was shocked by what Jesus said and went away sad. You see, he had many possessions. Jesus looked around at his disciples and said, "How hard it is for rich people to enter into the kingdom of God." The disciples were amazed at what he said, and then Jesus said it again, "How hard it is to enter the kingdom of God. It's easier for a camel to go through the eye of a needle than for a rich person to enter the kingdom of God." Then the disciples were even more amazed and asked each other, "Well, then, who can be saved?" Jesus looked at them and said, "It's impossible with humans, but not with God. All things are possible with God." Peter piped up and said, "Look, we've left everything to follow you." Jesus said, "It's true, anyone who leaves house or brothers or sisters or mother or father or children or fields on my behalf and for the sake of the gospel will receive one hundredfold in this day – houses and brothers and sisters and mothers and fathers and fields, along with persecutions. But, in the age to come, eternal life! Many who are first will be last and the last will be first."

When they were on the road going up to Jerusalem, Jesus was ahead of them. They were amazed, but some who were following were also afraid. Again, he took the disciples aside and began to tell them about the things that were going to happen to him – "Look! We're going up to Jerusalem, and the Son of Man will be handed over to the chief priests and the scribes, and they will condemn him to death, and deliver him to the Gentiles, and they will ridicule him and spit on him and whip him and kill him. After three days he will rise again from the dead."

James and John, Zebedee's boys, approached Jesus and said, "Teacher, we want you to do whatever we ask." He asked, "What do you want me to do for you?" They said, "Let us sit in your glory, one at your right hand and one at your left hand." Jesus said to them, "You don't know what you're asking. Can you drink the cup that I drink? Can you be baptized with my baptism?" They said, "We can!" Jesus said, "You're going to drink the cup that I drink and be baptized with my same baptism. To sit at my right or left? That's not up to me, but will be given to those for whom it has been prepared." Now, when the other ten disciples heard what James and John had asked Jesus, they were indignant. Jesus got them all together and said, "You know how the so-called 'rulers' of the Gentiles lord it over them and their great ones tyrannize them? Not so with you! Whoever wants to be great among you will be your servant, and whoever wants to be first among you will be servant of all. Why, even the Son of Man has come, not to be served but to serve, and to give his life as a means of release for many people."

They passed through Jericho. As they left Jericho accompanied by a large crowd, a blind beggar named

Bartimaeus (which means "Son of Timaeus") was sitting by the side of the road. When he heard it was Jesus the Nazarene who was approaching, he began to shout, "Son of David, Jesus, have mercy on me!" Many people in the crowd rebuked him and told him to shut up, but he only cried out even louder, "Son of David, have mercy on me!" Jesus stopped and said, "Call him." They called the blind man and said, "Cheer up! Get up! He's calling you." Bartimaeus threw down his cloak, jumped up, and went to Jesus. Jesus asked, "What do you want me to do for you?" The blind man said, "Rabbi, I want to see again." Jesus said to him, "Go, your faith has saved you." In a twinkling he saw again and followed Jesus on the road.

When they neared Jerusalem at Bethphage and Bethany, at the Mount of Olives, he sent two of his disciples ahead with these instructions, "Go into the opposite village and, in less than no time after you get there, you'll find a young donkey tied up. No one has ever ridden on it. Untie it and bring it to me. Someone is likely to ask you, 'What are you doing?' Don't worry, just say, 'The Lord needs it, and before you can say "Jack Robinson" he'll send it back.'" Sure enough, when they reached the village, they found a colt tied at the door outside in the street, so they untied it. Some folks who were standing there asked, "What do you think you're doing untying that donkey?" So, they told them exactly what Jesus had told them to say, and they let them untie the donkey. When they took the colt to Jesus, they laid their cloaks across its back and Jesus got on. Many other people spread their cloaks out on the road, while others went out into the fields, cut leafy branches, and laid them on the road before him. It was as if they were giving him the red-carpet treatment! The people in front of and behind him were all shouting, "Hosanna in the highest! Blessed is the one who comes in the name of the Lord! Blessed is the coming kingdom of our father David! Hosanna in the highest!" After he had entered Jerusalem, gone into the temple, and looked around at everything, he went back to Bethany with his twelve disciples because it was getting late in the day.

The next day, as they were leaving Bethany, he was hungry. Up ahead he saw a fig tree with some leaves sprouting. He went to see if he could find some figs to eat, but there weren't any, just some leaves. After all, it wasn't yet fig season. He said to the fig tree, "Nobody will ever eat fruit from you again, from this day forward." And his disciples heard it.

When they got to Jerusalem, he went into the temple and started to drive out the buyers and the sellers. He turned over the moneychangers' tables and the chairs of the dove merchants. He wouldn't let anyone carry anything through the temple. He was teaching, "Isn't it written, 'My house shall be called a house of prayer for all the nations?' But you have turned it into a cave of robbers!" When the chief priests and scribes heard him say this, they tried to figure out a way to kill him because they were afraid of him. Everybody was amazed at what he was teaching. Late in the day, when it was evening, they left the city.

The next morning, they walked by the fig tree and saw that it had withered. Peter remembered what Jesus had said the day before and said, "Rabbi, look! The fig tree you cursed is dried up." Jesus said to him, "Have faith in God. I tell you the truth, whoever says to this mountain 'Be taken up and thrown into the sea,' and doesn't doubt for a minute that what he says will happen, will see it happen. So, I tell you, all the things you pray for and seek, if you believe as if you have already received them, they will be yours. When you're praying and you remember that you need to forgive your neighbor, do it, so your heavenly Father will forgive your sins."

When they got to Jerusalem, he went to the temple again. As he was walking around, the chief priests, scribes, and elders approached him and asked, "By what authority are you doing these things? Who gave you the authority to do what you're doing?" In return, Jesus said, "Let me ask you a question. Answer me and I'll tell you by what authority I do these things. Was John's baptism from heaven or of human origin? Answer me!" They put their heads together and realized, "If we say 'From heaven,' he's going to ask us, 'Well, why didn't you believe him?' But if we say, 'Of human origin . . .'" The implications were clear. They were afraid of what the crowd would do if they heard that answer, because they all thought John was a prophet. So, they said to Jesus, "We don't know," and Jesus said, "Well, then, I'm not going to tell you by what authority I am doing these things."

He started to speak to them in parables. "A man planted a vineyard, put a hedge around it, dug a trough under the wine press, built a tower, leased it to some tenant farmers, and left home on a trip. At harvest time, he sent a slave to the tenant farmers to collect the fruits of the vineyard. They beat him and sent him away empty-handed. He sent a second slave, but the tenant farmers beat him over the head and abused him. They killed the third slave that the owner sent. On and on it went. They beat some and killed others. Finally, the man sent his beloved son. He figured, "Surely they will respect my son." But the farmers plotted, "This guy is the heir. Let's kill him and then we'll be the heirs and the property will be ours." They seized the son, killed him, and threw him out of the vineyard. What do you think the vineyard owner will do? He'll come home, destroy those tenant farmers, and give the vineyard to some other people. Haven't you read, 'A stone which the builders rejected, this stone has become the cornerstone; this is from the Lord, and it's marvelous in our eyes'?" They wanted to arrest him but, as before, they were scared of the crowd. They knew he had told the story against them. Instead of arresting him, they left and went away.

They sent some of the Pharisees and Herodians to try to trap him with a question. They approached him and said,

"Teacher, we know you are honest and don't show favoritism. You truly teach God's way. Is it lawful to pay Caesar's tax or not? Should we pay it or not?" Since he knew they weren't sincere and sensed their hypocrisy, he asked, "Why are you testing me? Bring me a coin to look at." They found one, showed it to him, and he asked, "Whose picture and inscription are on this coin?" When they said, "Caesar's," he said, "Well, in that case, give Caesar what belongs to Caesar and give God what belongs to God." They were completely amazed at his answer.

Some Sadducees came to him and asked a question about the resurrection, which was kind of ironic since they said there is no resurrection. "Teacher," they said, "Moses wrote that if someone's brother dies and leaves a wife but no children, the brother should marry the wife and have children for his brother. Now, there were seven brothers. The first one got married but died before they had children. The second brother married her and the same thing happened – right on down the line, with all of the brothers dying without having children. Finally, the woman died. Here's our question: In the resurrection, whose wife will she be if all seven of them had been married to her?" Jesus said, "Isn't this why you've lost your way, because you don't know the scriptures or the power of God? In the resurrection, they won't marry or be given in marriage, since they are as angels in heaven. Now, about the dead who are raised, haven't you read in the book of Moses how God spoke to him out of the bush and said, 'I am the God of Abraham and the God of Isaac and the God of Jacob'? God is not the God of the dead but of the living. You have really gotten off track!"

One of the scribes drew near and heard them arguing. When he realized how well Jesus answered them, he asked him, "Which commandment is first of all?" Jesus said, "The first is, 'Hear, Israel, the Lord our God is one Lord, and you are to love the Lord your God from your whole heart, self, mind, and strength.' This is a second commandment, 'Love your neighbor as you love yourself.' No commandment is greater than these two." The scribe replied, "Well said, Teacher, you have spoken the truth that he is one and there is no other. To love God from your whole heart, understanding, and strength, and to love your neighbor as yourself is greater than all of the burnt offerings and sacrifices." When Jesus heard the scribe's wise answer, he told him, "You're not far from the kingdom of God." After that, no one dared to asked him any more questions.

As he was teaching in the temple, Jesus asked, "Why do the scribes say the Christ is David's son? David himself said this when he was inspired by the Holy Spirit, 'The Lord said to my lord, "Sit down at my right hand, until I place your enemies under your feet."' David himself called him Lord, so how is he his son?" The great crowd liked what they were hearing.

When he taught, he warned, "Beware of the scribes who like to go around in their robes and be greeted in the marketplace. They also like having the seats of honor in the synagogues and at banquets. Yet, they prey on the widows and pray long, insincere prayers. I tell you, they'll receive a greater judgment in the end."

As he sat across from the temple treasury box, he watched the crowd throwing money in. Many rich people were putting in lots of money. He also saw a poor widow throw in two little coins, worth about a penny total. He called his disciples and said to them, "For sure, this poor widow put more in the treasury box than anybody and everybody else. All of them were giving from their discretionary income, but she put in everything she had. Even though she is poor, she gave away her whole livelihood."

As he was leaving the temple, one of his disciples said to him, "Teacher, look at these wonderful stones and buildings!" Jesus replied, "You see these great buildings?

Nothing will be left of them. Every stone will be torn down and they will all be destroyed."

Later, when he was sitting on the Mount of Olives across from the temple, Peter, James, and John privately asked him, "When is this going to happen? How will we know when all of these things are getting ready to happen?" Jesus said, "Be on guard so nobody leads you astray. Many others are going to come in my name. They'll say, 'I am,' and they'll lead you down the wrong path. But whenever you hear about wars or even rumors of wars, don't be alarmed. These things have to happen, but that doesn't mean the end is upon us. You see, nation will rise up against nation, kingdom against kingdom. There will be earthquakes in various places and famines. These are just the beginning, like labor pains. You'd better look out for yourselves, because they'll hand you over to local city councils. You'll be beaten in the synagogues and stand before rulers and kings. All of this will be for my sake, as your witness to me. But first the good news has to be proclaimed to the whole world.

"Whenever you are taken away and handed over, don't worry about what you're going to say. Say whatever is given to you to say. You see, it won't be you speaking but the Holy Spirit. Brother will betray brother to death. The same will hold true for a father and his children, and vice versa. You will be hated on account of your testimony to my name. But the one who endures to the end will be saved.

"When you see the desecrating object where it shouldn't be (Reader, be aware, take note, and understand!), the folks in Judea had better head for the hills. There won't be time to come down off the roof and get your affairs in order. If you're out working in your fields, don't go back to get your cloak. Oh, it's going to be terrible for the pregnant and nursing women when this happens. Just pray that it doesn't happen in the wintertime. When those days come, there's going to suffering such as the world has never seen since

God created it all – and such suffering will never be seen again. In fact, if the Lord had not limited those days, nobody would be saved. As it is, on account of God's elect, God did cut short the number of days.

"If anybody says, 'Look! Here is the Christ!' or 'Look! There is the Christ!', don't you believe it! You see, false Christs and prophets are going to appear. They'll do all sorts of signs and wonders to try to deceive God's elect, it at all possible. But I'm telling you, watch out! I've warned you about all these things. In those days, after the tribulation,

'The sun will be dark,

and the moon won't shine,'

and the stars will fall from heaven and the heavenly powers will be shaken. Then they will see the Son of Man coming on clouds with much power and glory. He will send his messengers to gather his elect from the four corners of the earth, all the way to heaven's boundary.

"You can learn a valuable lesson from the fig tree. When you see its tender branch and the leaves starting to sprout, you know summer's not far off. In the same way, whenever you see all these things happening, you know that it's near. Believe me, this generation won't pass away until all these things happen. Heaven and earth will pass away, but my words will never pass away.

"Nobody knows the day or time when all of this will happen, not even the angels nor the Son himself – only the Father knows. So, beware, stay alert, keep your eyes open, because you don't know when the appointed time is. Listen, it's like a man who left his house and authorized his servants to do their own work. He especially commanded the doorkeeper to watch out. So, you need to stay on your toes, because you don't know when the Lord of the house is coming. It might be late in the day. It might be at midnight or before the sun comes up. It might be early in the morning. Don't let him catch you asleep when he shows up unexpectedly! I'm telling everybody exactly what I'm telling you – Watch!"

Two days later it was time for the Passover Festival and the Feast of Unleavened Bread. The chief priests and scribes were trying to figure out how to arrest him deceitfully and then kill him. But, once again, they were afraid of the public reaction, so they said, "We'd better not do it during the festival; otherwise, the people will riot."

When he was visiting Simon the leper's house in Bethany, he was reclining at the table when a woman came in. She had an alabaster jar of very expensive oil of nard. She broke the jar and poured the oil on his head. Some of the people in the room were indignant and grumbled to each other, "Why did she waste this ointment? It could have been sold for a lot of money, almost a year's pay, and the money given to the poor." But Jesus said, "Leave her alone. Why are you bothering her? She has done a good work for me. You always have the poor with you, so whenever you want to help them, you can. But you won't always have me. She did what she could do. She prepared my body ahead of time for burial. I tell you the truth, wherever the gospel is preached in the whole world, what she has done for me will be told in her memory."

One of the twelve disciples, Judas Iscariot, went to the chief priests so he could betray Jesus to them. They were delighted and promised to pay him in silver coins. From that time on, Judas looked for the right moment to betray him.

On the first day of the Feast of Unleavened Bread, when they sacrificed the Passover lamb, his disciples asked him, "Where do you want us to prepare the Passover meal?" He sent two of his disciples with these instructions, "When you go into the city, a man carrying two water jars will meet you. Follow him. At whichever house he enters, say to the owner, 'The Teacher says, "Where is my guestroom where I can eat

Passover with my disciples?'" He will show you a large upstairs room that is already furnished. Get things ready for us there." When the disciples went into the city, things happened just as he had told them, and they prepared the Passover.

When evening came, Jesus arrived with the twelve. As they were reclining at the table and eating, Jesus said, "You can count on it, one of you eating with me is going to betray me." Naturally they were all very sad. One by one they said to him, "You can't mean me?" But he said, "It's one of you twelve, the one who is dipping his hand into the bowl with me. You see, the Son of Man will undergo what has been written about him, but woe to the man who betrays the Son of Man. It would have been better if he had never been born."

While they were eating, he took the bread, gave thanks, broke it, gave it to them, and said, "Take, this is my body." He then took a cup, gave thanks, and gave it to them. They all drank from the cup. He said, "This is my blood of the covenant which is poured out for many. Truly I tell you, I'll never drink from the fruit of the vine again until I drink it once more in the kingdom of God." Then they sang a hymn and went out to the Mount of Olives.

Jesus said to them, "All of you will be led into sin, because it is written,

'I will strike the shepherd,

and the sheep will be scattered.';

but after I have been raised up, I will go ahead of you to Galilee." But Peter told him, "Even if everybody else deserts you, I never will." Jesus said to him, "I tell you for sure, before a rooster crows twice tonight, you'll deny me three times." But Peter was adamant, "Even if it means I have to die with you, I will never, ever deny you." The rest of them said the same thing.

They arrived at a place called Gethsemane and he told his disciples, "Stay here while I pray." He took Peter, James, and John with him. He began to be very troubled and said to them, "My soul is deeply distressed to the point of death. Stay here and stay alert." Then he went on ahead a little way and fell down on the ground. He asked if it were possible for the things that were about to happen not to happen. But he said, "Abba! Father! All things are possible for you. Take this cup away from me. But not what I want, but what you want." When he went back, he found them sleeping and he asked Peter, "Simon, are you sleeping? What, you couldn't even stay awake and watch for one hour? Keep alert and pray that you won't be tempted. On the one hand, the spirit is willing, but on the other hand, the flesh is weak." He went away again and prayed the same things. When he came back a second time, he found them sleeping again. They couldn't keep their eyes open. They didn't know what to say to him. A third time he came and said, "Are you still sleeping and resting? It is enough. The time has come. Look, the Son of Man is being handed over to sinners. Get up! Let's go! See, my betrayer is here."

At that very minute, while he was speaking, Judas, one of the twelve disciples, arrived. A crowd from the chief priests, scribes, and elders was with him, armed with clubs and swords. The betrayer had given them this sign, "Seize the one I kiss and take him away." He came with all haste and said, "Rabbi." Then he kissed him. One of the bystanders drew his sword and cut off the ear of the slave of the high priest. Jesus said to them, "Have you come out to arrest me as an insurrectionist? Day in and day out I was teaching among you in the temple and you didn't seize me. But now you have come so the scriptures might be fulfilled." And they all fled and left him alone. A certain young man was following him. He was wearing a linen cloth. They grabbed him, but he shrugged off the cloth and ran away naked.

They forcefully led Jesus to the high priest. All of the chief priests, elders, and scribes had gathered. Peter followed him at a distance as far as the courtyard of the high priest. He sat down with the servants and warmed himself by the fire.

The chief priests and the entire Sanhedrin were looking for a witness to testify against Jesus so they could kill him, but they couldn't find one. There were many false witnesses, but they couldn't agree. Some of them lied about him. They said, "We heard him say, 'I will destroy this temple made by human hands and after three days I will build another not made by human hands.'" Again, their testimonies didn't agree.

The chief priest stood up in their midst and asked Jesus, "Don't you have anything to say? Why are these people testifying against you?" But he was silent. The chief priest again asked him, "Are you the Christ, the Son of the Blessed One?" Jesus said, "I am,

> and you will see the Son of Man
>
> seated on the right hand of power
>
> and coming on the clouds of heaven."

Then the chief priest ripped his robes and asked, "Why do we need any more witnesses? You heard the blasphemy. What do you think?" All of them condemned him and said he deserved to die. Some began to spit on him, cover his face, and strike him. They said, "Prophesy!" The guards hit him, slapped him, and took him away.

Down in the courtyard, one of the high priest's servant-girls saw Peter warming himself by the fire. She looked straight at him and said, "You were with the Nazarene Jesus." But he denied it, "I don't know what you're talking about." He went into an outer court and a rooster crowed. The servant-girl saw him again and said to the bystanders, "He's one of them!" He again denied it. A little while later, some bystanders said to Peter, "We're positive you're one of them. We can tell you're a Galilean." But he started to swear and curse and said, "I don't know this man you're talking about." And in no time, a cock crowed a second time. Peter remembered what Jesus had said, "Before a cock crows twice, you will deny me three times." And he broke down and began to weep.

As soon as morning came, the chief priests, along with the elders, the scribes, and the whole council, bound Jesus, led him away by force, and handed him over to Pilate, all according to their plan. Pilate asked him, "Are you the king of the Jews?" Jesus answered, "You say so." The chief priests accused him of many things. Pilate asked him, "Don't you have anything to say? They're accusing you of many things." But Jesus didn't say a word. Pilate was amazed.

At each festival, Pilate released one prisoner to them at their request. A prisoner named Barabbas was in prison with the insurrectionists because he had committed murder in the rebellion. So, the crowd rose up and asked him to do this for them. Pilate asked, "Do you want me to release the king of the Jews for you?" He knew the chief priests had handed him over because they were jealous. But the chief priests incited the crowd to ask Pilate to release Barabbas instead of Jesus. Again, Pilate asked them, "What do you want me to do with the man you are calling the king of the Jews?" They cried out, "Crucify him!" Pilate asked them, "Why? What evil did he do?" But they cried out even more loudly, "Crucify him!" Since Pilate wanted to keep the crowd happy and under control, he released Barabbas to them. After he had Jesus whipped, he handed him over to be crucified.

The soldiers led him away by force into the courtyard of the governor's headquarters and called the whole cohort together. They put a purple robe on him and placed a thorny crown on his head. The saluted him, "Greeting, king of the Jews!" They struck his head with a reed, spat on him, and knelt down and mock-worshiped him. After they had ridiculed him, they stripped off the purple robe, dressed him in his own clothes, and led him out to crucify him. They made a certain passerby, a guy named Simon, the father of Alexander and Rufus, a Cyrenian who was coming in from the field, carry his cross.

They took him to the place called Golgotha, which means "The Place of the Skull." They offered him wine mixed with myrrh, but he didn't take it. They crucified him and divided his clothes among them by casting lots to see who got what. They crucified him at 9:00 a.m. There was an engraved inscription of his charge, "The king of the Jews." They crucified two robbers with him, one on his right and one on his left.

Passersby insulted him, wagged their heads at him, and said, "Ha! You said you would destroy the temple and build it back in three days! Come down from the cross and save yourself!" The chief priests and the scribes were also ridiculing him, "He saved others, but he can't save himself! C'mon, Christ, king of Israel, come down from the cross. If we see that, we'll believe." The two others who had been crucified also insulted him.

When it was 12 noon, it was dark everywhere until 3:00 p.m. At 3:00 p.m., Jesus cried out with a great cry, "Eloi eloi lema sabachthani," which means, "My God, my God, why did you forsake me?" Some of the people standing around heard him and said, "Look! He's calling Elijah." Someone filled a sponge with sour wine, put it on a reed, gave it to him, and said, "Wait, let's see if Elijah comes to take him down." But Jesus gave a loud cry and died. The temple curtain was ripped in two from top to bottom. When the centurion standing across from him saw how he died, he said, "For sure, this man was the Son of God."

Now, there also were some women watching at a distance. The group included Mary Magdalene, Mary the mother of James the younger and Joses, and Salome. They had followed him and ministered to him when he was in Galilee. There were many others who had traveled with him to Jerusalem.

When evening came, since it was the Day of Preparation before the sabbath, Joseph of Arimathea, a respected member of the council who also was awaiting the kingdom of God, bravely asked Pilate for Jesus's body. Pilate was amazed that he was already dead, so he confirmed it with the centurion. When he was satisfied, he released the corpse to Joseph. He bought a linen burial cloth, took him down, wrapped him in the cloth, and laid him in a tomb cut into a rock. Then he rolled a stone against the entrance to the tomb. Mary Magdalene and Mary the mother of Joses saw where he was laid.

When the sabbath was over, Mary Magdalene, Mary the mother of James, and Salome bought spices so they could go to the tomb and anoint his body. Very early on Sunday morning, when the sun had risen, they went to the tomb. Along the way, they asked each other, "Who's going to roll the stone away from the tomb's entrance for us?" When they looked up, they saw that the very large stone had been rolled away.

When they went into the tomb, they saw a young man sitting on the righthand side. He was wearing a white robe. They were really frightened! But he said to them, "Don't be afraid! You're looking for Jesus the Nazarene who was crucified. He has been raised. He is not here! Look at the place where they laid him. But go and tell his disciples and Peter that he's going ahead of them into Galilee. They'll see him there, just as he said they would."

They left the tomb and ran away, trembling with amazement. But they didn't say anything to anyone because they were afraid . . .

WHAT NOW?

Now that you have read Mark's story as a whole and, perhaps, heard the story of Jesus in a new way, what does it mean for you?

Here are the things I asked you to look for as you read and listened to Mark's story. Take the time to write down your thoughts in light of what you heard Mark telling you about Jesus.

1.   What did the narrator/Mark tell you? Why?

2.   Think of Mark's story more as a portrait than a snapshot. Mark skillfully paints his portrait of who Jesus is and what Jesus means for your life. What do you see? Who is Jesus in Mark's gospel? Who is Jesus in your life?

3.   Why do you think Mark ends his story so abruptly, with the women fleeing from the tomb in fear and not telling anyone anything? How is this ending consistent with Mark's purpose for telling his story of Jesus? What do you think Mark wants you to do with what you've heard and learned about Jesus?

Mark took the time to share his story about Jesus. Is it a story that you're willing to share?